THE
SIN
NATURE

THE
SIN
NATURE

JIMMY SWAGGART

JIMMY SWAGGART MINISTRIES
P.O. Box 262550 | Baton Rouge, Louisiana 70826-2550
www.jsm.org

ISBN 978-1-941403-46-4

09-157 | COPYRIGHT © 2018 Jimmy Swaggart Ministries®

18 19 20 21 22 23 24 25 26 27 / EBM / 10 9 8 7 6 5 4 3 2 1

TABLE OF CONTENTS

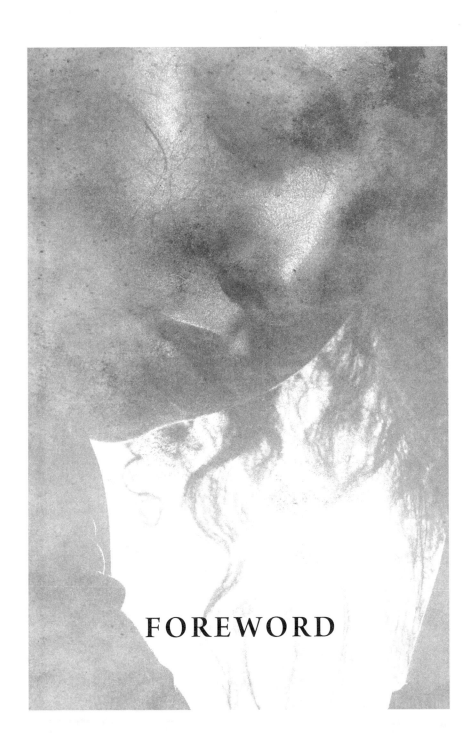

FOREWORD

FOREWORD

DESPITE THE FACT THAT the sin nature is one of the most important doctrines in the entirety of the Word of God, still, the modern church knows almost nothing about this particular doctrine.

In all my years of attending church, beginning as a young child, not one single time did I ever hear a message on the sin nature, or even hear it mentioned in any capacity.

Frances and I started in evangelistic work in the late 1950s. Every time we would go to a new town for a meeting, the next morning I would go to the used book shop in town and look for books concerning great preachers of the past. Over a period of time, I bought scores of these books and read them all. I never one time read one single message about the sin nature—never one time read an explanation of any nature. I probably saw the term once or twice, but there was never any explanation given, despite the fact that this is one of the most important doctrines in the Word of God. It is vitally significant that the believer understand it, but, regrettably, almost none do.

THE APOSTLE PAUL

It was Paul who gave us the rudiments of this great doctrine, but because of the translation from Greek to English, it is difficult to understand. I pray that the Lord will give us insight and help us to properly explain this that is so very important.

In fact, there are many doctrines in the New Testament that are of vital significance but, yet, are hardly understood at all by the modern church. I'll name a few:

- The doctrine of the curse of the broken law (Gal. 3:10).
- The doctrine of the flesh (Rom., Chpt. 8).
- The doctrine of spiritual adultery (Rom. 7:1-4).
- The doctrine of *"another Jesus"* (II Cor. 11:1-4).
- The doctrine of the Cross and sanctification (I Cor. 1:17-18, 2:2; Col. 2:10-15).
- The doctrine of how the Holy Spirit works (Rom. 8:2).

HOW TO LIVE FOR GOD

All of the doctrines that we have mentioned, and especially the sin nature, pertain to the manner in which we live for the Lord. The tragedy is that most Christians, although wondrously saved, have absolutely no idea of how to successfully live for the Lord. Consequently, the church makes up its own rules as it goes along, and almost all are wrong.

I realize that it sounds somewhat egotistical for me to make this statement: The modern church simply does not know how to live for God. But the sad fact is, that is the truth.

As a result, failure abounds on every hand, and as one man said to me the other day, "I just couldn't do it; it was too hard." Well, of course, the way that he was trying to do it, he was exactly right—it was too hard. In fact, just about all of the means and ways that man—and I should say the church—proposes pertain to the flesh, which opens the door for the sin nature to rule and reign in the heart and life of the believer. That is a tragedy!

THE RULING SIN NATURE

The sad fact (to which we have just alluded) is that the far greater majority of the modern church is ruled by the sin nature. Yes, they are saved, and many are Spirit-filled and actually being used by God, but, still, they don't know how to live for the Lord. With that being the case, failure is always the result. Also, one's spiritual growth is greatly stymied by this lack of knowledge. In Romans, Chapter 6, Paul mentions the words *know* or *knowing* four times. The sad fact is, as stated, for the most part, the modern Christian simply does not know.

I personally feel that as we go from chapter to chapter in this book, you will begin to see yourself, and more than likely, what you will see will not be pretty. In other words, you'll start to see why certain things happen and why certain things don't happen, and you'll see the reasons.

Jesus said, and I quote from the Expositor's Study Bible, including the notes: *"And you shall know the truth, and the truth shall make you free* (this is the secret of all abundant life in Christ;

the 'truth' is 'Jesus Christ and Him crucified,' which alone is the answer to the problems of man)" (Jn. 8:32).

Unfortunately, far too many believers simply don't know the truth. Truth you don't know can cause you great problems. Actually, truth is not a philosophy; rather it is a person, and that person is the Lord Jesus Christ:

- *"Jesus said unto him, I am the way, the truth, and the life"* (Jn. 14:6).
- *"Your word is truth"* (Jn. 17:17).
- *"And it is the Spirit who bears witness, because the Spirit is truth"* (I Jn. 5:6).

So, as stated, we find here that truth is not a mere philosophy. It is, in essence, a person.

There is a fountain filled with blood,
Drawn from Immanuel's veins;
And sinners plunged beneath that flood
Lose all their guilty stains.
Lose all their guilty stains,
Lose all their guilty stains.

The dying thief rejoiced to see
That fountain in his day,
And there have I, though vile as he,
Washed all my sins away.
Washed all my sins away,
Washed all my sins away.

Dear dying Lamb, Your precious blood
Shall never lose its power,
Till all the ransomed church of God
Be saved to sin no more.
Be saved to sin no more,
Be saved to sin no more.

E're since by faith I saw the stream
Your flowing wounds supply,
Redeeming love has been my theme,
And shall be till I die.
And shall be till I die,
And shall be till I die.

Then, in a nobler, sweeter song,
I'll sing Your power to save,
When this poor lisping, stammering tongue
Lies silent in the grave.
Lies silent in the grave,
Lies silent in the grave.

CHAPTER 1

JUSTIFICATION

JUSTIFICATION

"THEREFORE BEING JUSTIFIED BY FAITH, we have peace with God through our Lord Jesus Christ" (Rom. 5:1).

JUSTIFICATION

Unless one understands justification, one cannot understand the foundation of sanctification. As well, what this book is all about is that unless one understands the sin nature, it is impossible to understand the fullness of sanctification.

THEREFORE BEING JUSTIFIED BY FAITH

The heading presents Paul stating a scriptural fact. Kenneth Wuest said:

In coming to this place, Paul has clearly come to several conclusions. In Romans 1:18-3:20, he proves man's need for the righteousness of God. In Romans 3:21-30, he shows how such righteousness comes and how it is appropriated. In Romans 3:31-4:25, he shows by the example of Abraham and the testimony of David, that righteousness appropriated by faith does not upset, but rather establishes the spiritual order revealed in the Old Testament. In Romans, Chapter 5, which we will now address, the apostle now enlarges on the happiness and security of the justified, and especially on their assurance of God's love and of future blessedness.

WHAT THEN IS JUSTIFICATION?

Williams said, "It is the action of a judge declaring a prisoner innocent. The accused says nothing and does nothing. The judge is the sole actor—he justifies the man, i.e., he declares him righteous."

This beautiful work comes about as one expresses simple faith in Christ and what He did at Calvary and the resurrection.

Wuest also said, "Paul, by using the word *therefore*, points to a conclusion. In verses 1-8 of Romans, Chapter 4, he tells us that we are not justified by 'works.' In verses 9-12 of that same chapter, he adds 'ordinances' and then 'law obedience' in verses 13-25. These three things never give peace to the soul. It is faith alone that gives such peace!"

JUSTIFYING PEACE

Paul points here to justifying peace. In other words, it is a legal standing with God, which does not and, in fact, cannot change. There are two types of peace incumbent upon the believer: justifying peace and sanctifying peace.

Justifying peace is a peace with God and, as stated, is a legal standing—that which we are now studying.

There is enmity between God and unredeemed man. It is because of unconfessed and unrepented sin, and more particularly, it is because of the sinner's refusal to accept God's plan of redemption—the blood atonement of Jesus Christ (Rom. 8:7; Eph. 2:14-15). Enmity means "mutual hatred or ill will." The sinner does not want to have anything to do with God (Rom. 1:21-23), as well, *"God is angry with the wicked every day"* (Ps. 7:11).

In other words, because of sin, there is a war going on between God and unredeemed man; however, God feels the enmity far more than the sinner simply because it is God who has been wronged and offended, not man. So, as a result of this war, there is no peace between God and the sinner.

Actually, this very thing—a lack of peace with God—is the cause of all guilt and no doubt contributes to all manner of stress and mental disorders, as well as sickness and disease. As one doctor said, "I can remove the diseased physical organs, but, actually, that is only treating the symptoms. The root cause is something else." That something else is the enmity between God and man because of unconfessed, unrepented sin.

MAKING PEACE WITH GOD

When the sinner hears the Word of God and is convicted by the Holy Spirit, he is made to feel his wrong against God.

Consequently, this is where repentance comes in (Acts 20:21). Upon the sinner evidencing faith, all sin is washed away by the blood of Jesus, with the enmity instantly removed.

The new believer now has justifying peace, which is a result of justification. That is what is meant by the phrase, "making peace with God." This type of peace is abiding and never changes, which is what Paul is addressing here.

SANCTIFYING PEACE

This is the peace of God in the heart. While the first (justifying peace) has to do with justification, the second (sanctifying peace) has to do with sanctification (Rom. 8:6, 14:19; 15:13; Gal. 1:3).

As stated, the first is the result of a legal standing, with the second being the result of the work of the Holy Spirit. The first is static and never fluctuates, while the second changes almost from hour to hour. Every Christian has the first, but the second, every Christian may have.

AN EXAMPLE OF JUSTIFYING PEACE
AND SANCTIFYING PEACE

When Israel was told by Moses to apply the blood to the doorposts, this represented justifying peace (Ex., Chpt. 12).

One can well imagine that some Israelites that fateful night went to bed and slept well. That is sanctifying peace.

However, one can also imagine that many did not sleep well that night. While they had justifying peace, they did not have sanctifying peace. This was a lack of trust on their part, which robbed them of this peace. Yet, their justifying peace was not disturbed in the least, at least as long as they stayed in the house, because the blood was on the doorpost. As well, those who slept well were no less secure than those who paced the floor, or vice versa.

Sanctifying peace has to do with our trust in the Lord and is, as stated, up and down.

The more we grow in the Lord, however, the more we learn to trust Him, all of which has to do with sanctification and, therefore, our sanctifying peace.

Incidentally, "the Lord Jesus Christ" is the resurrection name of the Saviour, which guarantees our justification (Rom. 4:25).

The Greek word for peace is *eirene* and means "to bind together that which has been separated."

In other words (and getting back to justifying peace), our Lord made peace through the blood of the Cross (Col. 1:20). It is in the sense that through His atonement, He binds together again those who, by reason of their standing in the first Adam, had been separated from God. They, now, through faith in Christ, are bound again to God in their new standing in the last Adam— the Lord Jesus Christ.

This is justification. That is, a justified sinner has peace facing God. In other words, he can look God in the face because all sins have been washed away.

Wuest says, "He stands in the presence of God, guiltless and uncondemned and righteous in a righteousness which God accepts, in the Lord Jesus."

ACCESS FAITH

"By whom also we have access by faith into this grace wherein we stand, and rejoice in hope of the glory of God" (Rom. 5:2).

We might say that our whole being—not one aspect of it but all of it—has to be brought to the place of comprehending the love of God.

Immediately, when a man becomes spiritual by being born from above, the Bible becomes his authority.

The heading speaks of access to the throne of God at any time.

Jesus said, *"At that day you shall ask in My name: and I say not unto you, that I will pray the Father for you"* (Jn. 16:26).

This statement as made by Christ would have probably been better translated, "When you come before the throne of God in prayer to make a petition in My name, please know that you have instant and constant access to the Father, even as I. The Father grants you this because He loves you because you have loved Me and have believed that I came out from God."

Once the sinner comes to Christ, he is then made a new creation and, as well, a part of the family of God. Consequently, there are many privileges, with access to the throne being among that number.

This speaks of prayer, and more particularly, of intercession, which is instant access and can be gained on the spur of the moment at any place and time.

The word *access* in the Greek is *prosagoge* and refers to "a landing stage." The total idea of the word pertains to "access into and rest in; a haven or harbor."

This that Jesus did at Calvary and the resurrection provides so much more for the believer than most any of us even dare to think. Before Calvary, and due to the sin debt not yet having been paid, even the strongest of believers did not have the privileges in Christ that are now available to even the least child of God. Concerning this, Jesus lauded John the Baptist by saying of him, *"Among them who are born of women there has not risen a greater."*

Then He said, *"Notwithstanding he who is least in the kingdom of heaven is greater than he"* (Mat. 11:11). John the Baptist closed out the old covenant. Actually, he was the last prophet of that era. Jesus ushered in the new covenant, and, in fact, He is the new covenant. He gave it to us, with all of its greater privileges and blessings, solely because of the great price He had paid and the victories that He won. So, anyone in this new covenant is greater—as far as privileges are concerned—than anyone in the old covenant.

GRACE

The heading refers to the fact that the believer is set before the throne of God in a righteousness that is spotless, a life that is endless, and a dignity that is glorious.

All of the sins of the believer are canceled by God in the death of Christ; consequently, God has no sins to impute to Him. That matter has been eternally settled by Christ's sufficing atonement, and His resurrection attests the fact. There is, therefore, no longer any question regarding the believer's sins between him and God. That question—the sin question—was the looming, all-encompassing, and disturbing factor in relation to God, and Christ removed it according to the requirements of divine righteousness.

Jesus bore infinitely all the wrath of God due to sin and its fruit, and He satisfied and vindicated all the claims of the throne of God against man as a sinner, which was done at Calvary. That's the reason the Cross is the foundation of every Bible doctrine.

Consequently, this great salvation is, therefore, founded upon eternal righteousness and is the result of the divine activity operating in grace, which is a result of the Cross.

Williams says, "As stated, peace is the result of justification, and is, consequently, distinct from it. Faith enjoys this peace, and glories not only in salvation and all that it embraces, but in its Divine Author, God Himself."

Grace here is seen as a haven or harbor. The French have a word for this entrance or access. They call it *entrée*. It refers to one being brought before a potentate by a friend, who has properly attired him, in order to present him into the presence of the king.

That is exactly what Jesus does for a believing sinner—He cleanses Him in His own precious blood, clothes him with Himself in His righteousness, and brings him into the full favor (grace) of God the Father. As stated, this is entrée.

REJOICING

The heading portrays three things:

1. If the believer even halfway understands the tremendous privileges and favor afforded him as a result of his

standing in Christ, there will be a perpetual rejoicing in him. Man is a spiritual being, as well as physical and mental. As such, only God can truly satisfy the hunger and thirst of the soul. When He is given His rightful place in the believer's heart and life, as Peter said, it truly is *"joy unspeakable and full of glory"* (I Pet. 1:8).

2. The *"hope"* presented in Romans 5:2 does not mean that hope is that wherein we glory, but that being in a state of hope, we glory. The idea is that the future is guaranteed respecting these great things that God will do, but we do not know exactly when it will happen. This is our state of hope.

3. Finally, the *"glory of God"* is that which is coming. Even though we are given much evidence in the Word of God concerning that which is to come, still, it is so far beyond what we now see or know that one is little able to properly evaluate such coming glory. Consequently, Paul said, *"For now we see through a glass, darkly"* (I Cor. 13:12). The hope here is that of ultimately participating in the glory of heaven, which we most definitely shall.

AND NOT ONLY SO, BUT WE GLORY IN TRIBULATIONS ALSO

"And not only so, but we glory in tribulations also: knowing that tribulation works patience" (Rom. 5:3).

If we are to concentrate on the Lord, we must mortify our religious self-will.

When a man is born from above, he has a new internal standard, and the only objective standard that agrees with it is the Word of God as expressed in the Bible.

The heading does not simply mean *when* we are in tribulations, but also, *because* we are in tribulations, with the tribulations being the ground of the glorying. To be sure, this requires supernatural grace supplied by the Holy Spirit.

It is not that Paul was exulting or that we are to exult because of the tribulations themselves, but it is because of their beneficial effect upon the Christian life. This, the saint must learn to do. We must learn to look at these trials and difficulties as assets that develop the Christian character.

The word *tribulations* in the Greek is *thlipsis* and means "a pressing, pressing together, pressure, oppression, affliction, distress, straits." Wuest says, "In the Greek text, it is preceded by the definite article (the tribulations), marking these out as things naturally expected in a Christian life."

We are to perceive how they serve for our probation now: they test our endurance, and proved endurance increases hope.

Pulpit says, "The idea is that tribulations test, and endurance under them proves, the genuineness of faith."

TRIBULATION AND THE MODERN GOSPEL

Much of the so-called modern faith teaching denies any and all tribulations for the believer, claiming that such are basically brought about because of a lack of faith or proper confession. Of course, such teaching defies not only the peripheral aspects of the gospel but, actually, its very core. Not a one of these teachers (at least those of whom I am aware) would even think of quoting the statement of Paul concerning the glorying in tribulations, or else, they would define tribulations in an improper manner. The tribulations came to Paul and come to all true believers, not because of a lack of faith, but because of great faith.

Actually, I think the Scripture plainly teaches: The greater the faith, the greater the tribulations. Job, whom we will address momentarily, is an excellent example.

RIGHT AND WRONG TRIBULATIONS

The types of tribulations that Paul addresses here are mostly those which come to us via the spirit world, in other words, the attacks of Satan. As should be obvious, the Evil One is bitterly opposed to the believer's work for the Lord and his walk with the Lord. Consequently, he attacks with temptation, with traps, and at times, with oppression, which can lead to depression.

I suppose every believer in history has suffered spiritual oppression at one time or the other. It's as if a hundred pounds is placed on one's shoulders only to get heavier. It's like a darkness that descends on a person, and there is no light, which means there is no hope.

Concerning this and concerning oppression, the Bible says: *"How God anointed Jesus of Nazareth with the Holy Spirit and with power: who went about doing good, and healing all who were oppressed of the devil; for God was with Him"* (Acts 10:38).

Oppression can cause mental disorder, emotional disorder, and certain types of illnesses, and, as stated, can lead to depression.

WHAT IS THE CURE?

Pure and simple, the cure is the Cross of Christ (I Cor. 1:17-18; 2:2; Gal. 6:14; Col. 2:10-15).

Sometime ago while preaching on a Sunday morning at Family Worship Center, I was addressing this very subject. All of a sudden, it dawned on me that since the Lord began to open up to me the great Message of the Cross, which began to take place sometime in 1997, I haven't suffered one moment of oppression from then until now. At the time of this writing, that has been some 20 years. Before that, it was almost a common occurrence, which, needless to say, made life miserable.

Satan was defeated at Calvary's Cross, and that goes for all of his minions of darkness, whether demon spirits or fallen angels. If the believer will place his or her faith exclusively in Christ and what Christ has done for us at the Cross, and maintain it exclusively in Christ and the Cross, the Holy Spirit will then go to work within such a life, and everything will change for the better. To be blunt, the Cross of Christ is the answer, and the only answer, for everything. It is there where our Lord atoned for all sin, paid the price for all that we have, and, as well, defeated all the powers of darkness. This is God's way, and His only way, simply because no other way is needed.

To be sure, tribulation can come to us via other people. Many times, if not most of the time, it is from those who claim to be believers. Nevertheless, the powers of darkness are behind that as well.

TRIBULATION AS THE RESULT OF WRONGDOING

To be sure, such will most definitely occur if we take a wrong path, a path of sin, or a path of wrong doctrine.

Paul said, concerning this very thing, *"My son, despise not you the chastening of the Lord, nor faint when you are rebuked of Him: For whom the Lord loves He chastens, and scourges every son whom He receives"* (Heb. 12:5-6).

While such tribulation is most definitely grievous, still, it is meant for our good, for Paul also said: *"But He* (the Lord chastens) *for our profit, that we might be partakers of His holiness. Now no chastening for the present seems to be joyous, but grievous: nevertheless afterward it yields the peaceable fruit of righteousness unto them which are exercised thereby"* (Heb. 12:10-11).

KNOWING THAT TRIBULATION WORKS PATIENCE

The heading points to the characteristics of a man who is unswerved from his deliberate purpose and his loyalty to faith and piety by even the greatest trials and sufferings.

The word *works* in the Greek is *katergazomai* and means "to accomplish, achieve, to do that from which something results." So, the tribulation is to generate or produce patience.

The word *patience* in the Greek is *hupomone* and means "steadfastness, constancy, endurance."

It also has reference to "remaining under," thus, to remain under trials in a God-honoring way so as to learn the lesson they are sent to teach, rather than attempt to get out from under them in an effort to be relieved of their pressure.

So, we can see from all of this how that the Holy Spirit is directing and orchestrating all events, some which seem to be hurtful to the flesh, but all which are invigorating to the spirit.

AND PATIENCE, EXPERIENCE

"And patience, experience; and experience, hope" (Rom. 5:4).

The heading points to an end result.

The word *experience* in the Greek is *dokimen* and means "the result of trial, approvedness" (Phil. 2:22). It is a "tried integrity, a state of mind that has stood the test." This is done for the purpose of proving and finding that the person tested meets the specifications in order for approval to be put upon him. Its results are a spiritual state that has shown itself proof under trial.

The spiritual mettle of the believer must be tested exactly as any product is tested respecting its veracity. The idea is not that God is to see what the test brings forth, for He already knows. The test is carried out for the benefit of the believer. It shows us where we are, and we generally find that we are much weaker than we thought.

The problem of self-reliance rears its ugly head in the believer just as it does in the unbeliever. Unfortunately, this ever-present problem cannot be rooted out by the laying on of hands or by the manifestation of any of the gifts of the Spirit.

In the natural these things are somewhat similar to a computer program that says that an instrument or piece of equipment should function in a certain way. Irrespective, the equipment still must be put to the test before it can be released to the public.

Spiritually, we know what salvation does. The instructions are given to us in the Word of God; however, it is only when we are put to the test that we actually know how well that we have allowed these great qualities to function within our lives. Finding out our weaknesses, which tests will always bring out, keeps the believer humble and on his knees.

AND EXPERIENCE, HOPE

The heading presents the natural product of an approved experience.

Wuest says, "The experience of what God can do, or rather of what He does, for the justified amid the tribulations of this life, animates into new vigor the hope with which the life of faith begins."

A disapproved experience generates no hope whatsoever, as would be obvious. However, when one is put to the test and there finds that the grace of God is sufficient for all things, such causes hope to spring forth.

Williams says, "Job illustrates the discipline of verses 3 and 4. He exercised patience and so had the experience, or proof, that the issue of the divine action is that God is full of pity and of tender mercy (James 5:11), so that he could boast of the tribulations which had disciplined him, and rejoice in the hope that made him not ashamed."

AND HOPE MAKES NOT ASHAMED

"And hope makes not ashamed; because the love of God is shed abroad in our hearts by the Holy Spirit which is given unto us" (Rom. 5:5).

The heading tells us that this is not a false hope. It will not shame us in the end as being baseless and without fulfillment. As we have previously said, the type of hope mentioned here is guaranteed of fulfillment, with the only question being as to the fullness of time.

To the contrary, the type of hope that characterizes the world is the exact opposite. To be frank, the world never fulfills its promises simply because it has no ways or means to do so. The system of the world is of Satan, and he is a liar and the father of it. Consequently, all he can do is lie because there is no truth in him (Jn. 8:44). Therefore, there is no hope in anything Satan does. I realize that's a powerful statement, but it happens to be true.

BECAUSE THE LOVE OF GOD IS SHED ABROAD IN OUR HEARTS

Concerning this, Denney says, "The above statement by Paul proclaims that all these Christian experiences and hopes rest upon an assurance of the love of God. It is obvious from verse 5 and the whole connection, that the love of God to us is meant and not our love to Him. It is the evidence of God's love to us which the apostle proceeds to set forth."

THE AGAPE KIND OF LOVE

This love tells us that everything God allows to come upon us is for our good and not our hurt, irrespective of the difficul ties of the moment.

This love of which Paul speaks is *agape,* and speaks of a love that is awakened by a sense of value in an object that causes one to prize it. It springs from an apprehension of the preciousness of an object. It is a love of esteem and approbation. The quality of this love is determined by the character of the one who loves, in this case the Lord Himself, and that of the object loved.

Consequently, God's love for a sinful and lost race springs from His heart in response to the high value He places upon each human soul. Every sinner is exceedingly precious in His sight.

THE PHILEO KIND OF LOVE

The Greek word *phileo* is another word for love. It is a love that is the response of the human spirit to what appeals to it as pleasurable. Such type of love will not do here, for there is nothing in a lost sinner in which the heart of God can find pleasure, but on the contrary, everything that His holiness rebels against.

However, even though there is nothing in the sinner that is pleasurable to God, but rather the very opposite, still, each sinner is most precious to God. First of all, it is because the sinner bears the image of his Creator, even though that image is marred by sin, and second, because through redemption, that sinner can be conformed into the very image of God's dear Son.

This preciousness of each member of the human race to the heart of God is the constituent element of the love that gave His Son to die on the Cross. The degree of the preciousness is measured by the infinite sacrifice that God made.

The love in John 3:16, for instance, is a love whose essence is that of self-sacrifice for the benefit of the one loved. This love is based upon an evaluation of the preciousness of the one loved.

THE EROS KIND OF LOVE

The Greek word *eros* speaks of a type of love that can only be described as self-serving. This type of love is extended to individuals, providing they are of some merit. In other words, the person is loved because he or she is rich, famous, or of some supposed worth or value. The idea is that when the worth or value is no longer there, the person is no longer desired.

The Holy Spirit thought so little of this type of love that it is not once mentioned in the New Testament. One can well understand why—it is the very opposite of agape love.

Regrettably, this type of love characterizes the world and even, sad to say, much of the church. If the person makes the system look good, the world showers accolades on that individual; however, when that ceases to be the case, the person is discarded like a broken piece of furniture.

Regrettably, as stated, many churches fall into the same category. If the person is wealthy, famous, or of some supposed value, he is a welcomed member; however, if that ceases to be the case, in too many churches, the individual is no longer wanted or desired. Consequently, far too often the very ones who need what true Christianity provides are left out in the cold for the simple reason that they do not make the church look good.

I hope the reader can see how utterly ungodly such an attitude and spirit are. As stated, this is the very opposite of the true love of God. The preachers in these churches must realize that when God saved them (that is, if they are saved), there was absolutely nothing in them of any worth or value to the Lord. He loved them simply for their sake alone and nothing else. In turn, we must evidence the same type of love toward others, even those who are the most unlovable.

The words, *"is shed abroad,"* in the Greek text is *ekcheo* and means "to pour out, or has poured in, and keeps pouring in."

Inasmuch as the love of God keeps pouring into our hearts, likewise, it is meant to pour out of our hearts onto others. If it doesn't, the implication is that the flow will cease from God to us. As it was shed abroad to us, it is meant to be shed abroad by us to others.

As well, this love must never be diluted lest it mean something else altogether. It must remain the same type of love given to us by God—the God kind of love.

A DEMONSTRATION OF THE LOVE OF GOD

Jesus Christ is the greatest personification of the love of God. As someone has said, "He is love incarnate and personified (I Jn. 3:16); in fact, is God's self-revelation."

Jesus is not recorded in Matthew, Mark, or Luke, as using the word *agape* to express God's love for men. Rather, He revealed it by His countless acts of compassionate healings (Mk. 1:41; Lk. 7:13), His teaching about God's acceptance of the sinner (Lk. 15:11-32; 18:10-14), His grief-stricken attitude to human disobedience (Mat. 23:37; Lk. 19:41), and by being Himself a friend of sinners and outcasts (Lk. 7:34).

In other words, He did not talk so much about it, but rather revealed it, which is the exact opposite of many of us Christians.

This saving activity is declared in John's writings to be a demonstration of the love of God, imparting an eternal reality of life to men (Jn. 3:16; I Jn. 4:9). The whole drama of redemption, centering as it does on the death of Christ, is divine love in action (Rom. 5:8; II Cor. 5:14; Gal. 2:20).

MAN'S LOVE FOR GOD

Man's natural state is to be God's enemy (Rom. 5:10; Col. 1:21) and to hate Him (Lk. 19:14; Jn. 15:18), with this enmity being seen for what it is in the crucifixion.

In other words, if one wants to know what man thinks of God, one only has to look at the crucifixion, and the enmity becomes crystal clear.

However, the manner in which this hatred of man toward God is changed is always brought about by the love of God. In other words, God loves man into accepting Him as Saviour, etc. Even acts of judgment are, in reality, the love of God, even though unregenerate man thinks the opposite.

In applying pressure and using whatever capacity to do so, such is meant to bring man to his spiritual senses, which it sometimes does. To be sure, that is God's love in action, even though it may be painful for the moment.

A PERSONAL EXAMPLE OF JUDGMENT THAT WAS LOVE

When my parents heard the gospel of Jesus Christ for the first time, I was only 5 years old. Sadly, even as so many others, they rebelled against the pleas of the Holy Spirit and refused to accept the Lord as their Saviour. They even thought they could pull up stakes in our hometown and go to a distant city and things would be different.

They did not realize that they were under conviction by the Holy Spirit, and wherever they went or whatever they did, this conviction would remain. It did exactly that.

The memory of the morning we left our home in Louisiana is freeze-framed in my mind. I might quickly add that we were not only leaving our home, we were leaving the church where my parents had first heard the gospel. My mother and dad were going to South Texas where my dad hoped to go into business. The year was 1940.

Things did not go well in Texas for the simple reason that my mother and dad were running from God. It was a trek that one could not hope to win.

Very shortly after arriving in that beautiful area, my baby brother, who was only a few months old, contracted pneumonia. This was before the days of the wonder drugs; however, inasmuch as the hand of God was in all of this, I don't think the drugs would have mattered anyway.

Once again, I remember it distinctly. We were living in a small tourist court. Much of the day, I had been at the hospital with my dad where my baby brother had been taken. My mother, as well, had come down with pneumonia and was herself hospitalized.

THE SOMBER WORD

Sometime that night, my dad and I went back to the tourist court and went to bed. At about daylight there was a knock at the door.

I awakened along with my dad, that is, if he had ever been asleep. I remember distinctly his raising up in the bed and asking who was at the door. The voice of my uncle came through the door, with dad instantly arising and opening the door for him to come in.

My uncle just stood there for a few moments saying nothing, with my dad looking at his face. Once again, this moment is freeze-framed in my mind. My dad looked at my uncle and said to him, "It's Donnie, isn't it?" That was my brother's name.

My uncle dropped his head, and his voice broke as he said, "He died about an hour ago."

I do not remember what my dad said or did at that time as that is lost from my memory. However, I distinctly remember the funeral that took place, I suppose the next day. The casket was tiny inasmuch as my baby brother was only a few months old, but I'll never forget seeing him that last time. When I was a kid, my hair was so blonde that it was almost white. By contrast, my brother's hair was jet black and in ringlet curls all over his head.

THE FUNERAL

The only ones at the funeral were the morticians and an Assembly of God pastor, with the short service being conducted at the gravesite.

Inasmuch as we had just arrived in this part of the world, I have no idea how this pastor knew my parents. My mother was not there because she was too sick to come.

I remember the pastor and the mortician helping my dad out of the car and walking with him to the gravesite. Being only 5 years old, I really did not understand the terrible reality of death and what it meant, but this I do remember: After the short service, they opened the casket the last time, and my dad looked at my baby brother lying in the casket. He bent over that small form and said to him, "I promise you, I will meet you in heaven."

A few days later when my mother was able to travel, my parents went back to our home in Louisiana to the church that they had left, and a short time later, they made Jesus the Saviour and Lord of their lives.

Even though the death of my baby brother was of great sorrow, still, it was the hand of God bringing my parents to their senses in order that they would say yes to Him, which they did. As stated, even though it was hurtful for the time, that which was done was the love of God, and it must always be understood as such, which should be obvious to all.

BY THE HOLY SPIRIT WHICH WAS GIVEN TO US

The heading plainly proclaims that this great attribute of God shed abroad in our hearts is altogether a work of the Holy Spirit. In fact, every single thing received by man from God in any capacity is always through and by the person, office, agency, work, and ministry of the Holy Spirit.

I realize that many Greek scholars claim that the mention of the Holy Spirit in this fashion has nothing to do with the Acts 2:4 experience, but is rather the act of regeneration carried out by the Spirit in the heart and life of the believing sinner. In fact, that is true up to a point, but not altogether. While it is true that the Holy Spirit definitely comes into the believer's heart and life at conversion, still, it is not true that this is the entirety of His work.

Actually, if the believer does not go on and be baptized with the Holy Spirit according to Acts 2:4, while the Holy Spirit certainly is in his heart and life, one could say without fear of exaggeration that in this mode, He (the Holy Spirit) is pretty much helpless. It is only when the believer is baptized with the Holy Spirit, which is always accompanied by the speaking with other tongues (Acts, Chapters 2, 8, 9, 10, 19), that He is then given the latitude to properly do His office work in the heart and life of the believer. The book of Acts graphically portrays this.

Regrettably, there are many who actually have been baptized with the Holy Spirit (even most, one could say) but still have not allowed Him the latitude and control He must have in order to do His complete work. However, this is not the fault of the Spirit, but rather of the person.

THE CROSS OF CHRIST AND THE HOLY SPIRIT

The believer must understand that the Holy Spirit works exclusively within the parameters, so to speak, of the finished work of Christ. In other words, it's the Cross of Christ that gives the Holy Spirit the legal means to do all that He does (Rom. 8:2). This means that the believer must have his or her faith exclusively in Christ and the Cross, and maintain it exclusively in Christ and the Cross. Unfortunately, most believers understand the Cross of Christ relative to salvation, but they have no idea whatsoever of the part the Cross of Christ plays in our sanctification. In other words, they don't understand the Cross relative to how we live for God, how we order our behavior, or how we obtain victory over the world, the flesh, and the Devil (Rom. 8:1-11; I Cor. 1:17-18; 2:2; Col. 2:10-15).

As well, I think one cannot really understand the love of God unless one understands the Cross of Christ not only for salvation but, as well, for sanctification. This is how the Holy Spirit works.

Regrettably and sadly, virtually the entirety of all believers in the world are presently being ruled by the sin nature simply because they do not understand the great truth that I am attempting to address briefly at this time.

VICTORY...

Most believers try to attain victory over the world, the flesh, and the Devil by all types of means—none of which are scriptural. While certain things may be scriptural in their own right, they become unscriptural when we try to use them to overcome the flesh. I speak of fasting, which is definitely scriptural, but it was never meant to give one victory over sin, and, in fact, cannot give one victory over sin. I also speak of one's prayer life, which every believer most definitely ought to have; however, one cannot pray one's way to victory. It just simply cannot be done.

Everything we receive from the Lord—and I mean everything—all and without exception is made possible by the Cross of Christ. That's how important this is. We as believers must have the constant help of the Holy Spirit. We can only have that help if we place our faith exclusively in Christ and the Cross.

Let me say it once again: The Holy Spirit works exclusively within the framework of the finished work of Christ. In other words, it's the Cross that gives the Holy Spirit the legal means to do all that He does with us and for us. It is the Cross that has made it possible.

Before the Cross, the Holy Spirit could come into the hearts and lives of only a few people, such as prophets, etc. When His work was complete, He would leave. Now, due to the Cross, the Holy Spirit comes into the heart and life of each and every believer at conversion. Why could not He do such before the Cross? He could not simply because the blood of bulls and goats could not take away sins, so that means the sin debt remained, and the Holy Spirit cannot function in sin in any capacity. When the Cross was a fact—that meant that all sin was atoned at least for all who would believe—then it was made possible for the Holy Spirit to come into our hearts and lives and to abide forever. So, whenever believers try to gain victory in any way other than faith in Christ and the Cross, such constitutes an insult to the Lord and to the great price that Jesus paid at Calvary. Once we think a moment, it then becomes clearer.

For instance, there are many people, such as elderly people, who cannot fast. As well, there are some who, due to illness and weakness, cannot function in a state of intercessory prayer unending. They simply can't do it. Anything and everything that God does can be enjoyed by every single person who desires to do so. All that is required is that our faith be exclusively in Christ and the Cross, which then gives the Holy Spirit latitude to work. That, and that alone, brings the victory.

He pardoned my transgressions,
He sanctified my soul,
He honors my confessions,
Since by His blood I'm whole.

He keeps me every moment
By trusting in His grace;
'Tis through His blest atonement,
That I may see His face.

He brings me through affliction,
He leaves me not alone;
He's with me in temptation,
He keeps me for His own.

He prospers and protects me,
His blessings ever flow;
He fills me with His glory,
He makes me white as snow.

He keeps me firm and faithful
His love I do enjoy,
For this I shall be grateful,
And live in His employ.

There's not a single blessing
Which we receive on earth
That does not come from heaven,
The source of our new birth.

It is truly wonderful what the Lord has done!
It is truly wonderful! It is truly wonderful!
It is truly wonderful what the Lord has done!
Glory to His name.

CHAPTER 2

WITHOUT
STRENGTH

WITHOUT STRENGTH

"FOR WHEN WE WERE yet without strength, in due time Christ died for the ungodly" (Rom. 5:6).

FOR WHEN WE WERE YET WITHOUT STRENGTH

The heading pertains to an extremely negative scenario respecting the unbeliever.

First of all, this passage proclaims, in effect, the doctrine of total depravity. The sinner does not know God, does not understand God, and does not understand anything about God. In fact, the apostle also states that the sinner is *"dead in trespasses and sins"* (Eph. 2:1), and dead is dead. In fact, the sinner is constantly at war with God, whether he realizes it or not.

In this state the sinner is helpless, unable to reach God, and actually little believes in God, if at all! As well, he is so blinded spiritually that he has no idea how despicable his true state actually is. Whatever that state is, in his mind, he thinks he has the necessary resources to correct it, whether with education, money, ability, or even brute force.

In the Greek, "without strength" is *asthenes* and means "feeble, impotent, sick, weak," which refers to such in the spiritual sense.

All of this means that God had to reach man, for man had no way to reach God. Absolutely void of any true spirituality, it is impossible for him to recognize or understand his true state. Consequently, the only way this spiritual death can be awakened is for the Word of God to be ministered unto the sinner, with the Holy Spirit energizing that Word, which seizes upon the heart of the person and places him under conviction. For the first time, he then begins to realize his undone state. That is the reason the preaching of the gospel is so very, very important (Mk. 16:15).

IN DUE TIME CHRIST DIED FOR THE UNGODLY

The heading declares the nature of God's love.

Man can sacrifice himself when he thinks he has an adequate motive, as is evidenced in war. However, the unique character of God's love is displayed in the fact that Christ died for men when there was no motive to move Him to do so, but every reason to the contrary. Man is morally impotent and actively ungodly, sinful, and hostile.

It was God's own heart that prompted Him to pity and to redeem lost men. God could not possibly have found in us any adequate reason or a moral worthful enough to justify His action. This is clear from the declaration regarding man's impotency, ungodliness, sinfulness, and hostility.

No non-Christian would knowingly lay down his life for a Nero or a Hitler. Consequently, the extraordinary character of God's love is seen in that Christ died for the temporal and eternal welfare of men who hated Him.

In the entirety of this Scripture, the context clearly indicates what is meant: *substitution*. Thus, our Lord died instead of us, and took our penalty on behalf of us, in that His death was all for us. And yet, what I've just stated does not adequately explain it. The truth is, even if we had died on a cross, our sacrifice would have been unacceptable because it would have been polluted, as should be obvious. A perfect sacrifice was absolutely necessary, and only Christ could provide such.

IN DUE TIME

The words *due time* in the Greek is *kairos* and means "a strategic time, a time determined by a set of circumstances that make that particular point of time part of the efficient working of an action or set of actions."

In fact, considering that the promise of the coming Redeemer was given immediately after the fall of man in the garden of Eden (Gen. 3:15), why was Jesus some 4,000 years in coming? That is a long time!

We learn from the words *due time* that there was, in effect, a specific time—ordered by events—in which this great plan of redemption could be carried out.

Among other things, this terrible delay or length of time before the first advent of Christ tells us how awful and terrible that sin really is. Even though God could speak worlds into existence, He could not simply decree redemption, but He, in fact, had to carry out a certain order of events before this great thing could be done.

This is what makes it so absolutely unreasonable and even pitiful for the church to think that humanistic wisdom, such as psychology, would have any bearing whatsoever on this dread malady called sin. It took the death of Christ on the Cross, along with His resurrection, to satisfy the claims of heavenly justice and to break the grip of sin. If that is true, and it is, how does poor mortal man, who is fallen himself, think that he can effect any type of cure, healing, or deliverance?

THE FIRST ADVENT OF CHRIST

For the first advent of Christ, certain things had to be in place. Jesus not only had the task of redeeming mankind, but He, as well, had to take back His title and position of king of Kings, which had been usurped by Satan, at least on earth. Satan, as the god of this world, had become such by the default of Adam and Eve. As the first Adam had lost his way, the last Adam would have to establish that way again. Jesus would do this as a man, which was of necessity, and not as God, but yet, never ceasing to be God.

A particular people would have to be raised up through whom the Redeemer would come, which was Israel. A particular throne would have to be established in order for kingship to be regained. That throne was the throne of David. As well, the throne lineage had to play out until the Romans ruled the world, at least at that day. This was necessary for several reasons.

It had been prophesied by Daniel that the rule of the Romans would be the *due time* (Dan. 7:7; 9:24-26).

As we have already stated, the salvation of man was and is far more complex than meets the eye, and even that is a gross understatement. Man has to somehow come to the end of himself before he will finally admit his need for God. Even as this is true on an individual basis, it is also true respecting the entirety of mankind.

Consequently, man had to exhaust his mental resources respecting his philosophical quests. These ripened under the Greeks with their philosophy, but they did not and, in fact, *could not* satisfy the thirst of the human heart. It took some 4,000 years for all of this to be brought about.

Rome now ruled with its universal language and universal power. This was the time prophesied by Daniel. As degraded and evil as it was, the world was now ready—it was *due time.*

FOR SCARCELY FOR A RIGHTEOUS MAN WILL ONE DIE

"For scarcely for a righteous man will one die: yet peradventure for a good man some would even dare to die" (Rom. 5:7).

The heading has Paul using the word *righteous*, not in the usual New Testament sense, but in its normal meaning—a type of human goodness, at least as the world describes such. Paul is saying that a few might die for such a man.

YET PERADVENTURE FOR A GOOD MAN
SOME WOULD EVEN DARE TO DIE

The heading puts the situation on a slightly higher plane.

In other words, once every several centuries, a man may arise who would attempt to do right for the betterment of others, and he would be labeled by the world as "good." Down through the centuries, some have died for such a man, but such is rare.

Even though Paul is not actually addressing such at this time, it might be proper at this juncture to call attention to the untold millions who have willingly laid down their lives for the Lord Jesus Christ.

During the time of the early church, Rome made the floors of her sporting arenas slippery with blood. One might quickly add that it was blood shed by untold thousands of Christians who laid down their lives for Christ. It was demanded of them that they simply say, "Caesar is lord," and to do so would instantly grant them pardon. However, as simple as this was, the takers were few, with untold numbers saying instead, "Jesus is Lord." History is replete with the truth that they paid with their lives.

The same could be said for the Dark Ages when Roman Catholicism attempted to further its perverted version of the kingdom of God by torture and the sword. Only God knows the uncounted numbers who paid the full price for their allegiance to the Lord Jesus Christ. Their number, known only to God, will one day stand in splendor in the portals of glory, having died for His cause.

It must be quickly asked: Does anyone seriously think that these untold millions would have willingly laid down their lives, even as they did, for an imposter? I think it should go without saying that these millions did not and, in fact, would not have died for such a man. They died for their Redeemer, even though man, but yet, God.

BUT GOD COMMENDS HIS LOVE TOWARD US

"But God commends His love toward us, in that, while we were yet sinners, Christ died for us" (Rom. 5:8).

The heading pertains to the fact that Christ dying for the ungodly is a proof of love immeasurably beyond what is common among men. To say it another way: it is that the love of God toward ungodly men was displayed in the death of Christ.

Wuest said, "*Commends* in the Greek is *sunistemi* and means 'to put together by combining or comparing, hence, to show, prove, establish, exhibit.'"

He went on to say, "How greatly is this utmost love of man surpassed by the love of God."

Another expositor called attention to the fact that the word *commends* is in the present tense, meaning that God continuously establishes His love in that the death of Christ remains as its most striking manifestation.

So, Calvary ever remains at the forefront of God's thought toward man, even grossly wicked, ungodly, and sinful man. Whatever it is that men think of God, they only have to look at Calvary to know who and what God really is, and more particularly, who and what He is toward them. There is no way that His love could be better or more visibly displayed than by that single act of giving Himself as a sacrifice on Calvary so long ago.

IN THAT, WHILE WE WERE YET SINNERS, CHRIST DIED FOR US

The heading points to the fact that Jesus died for those who are at enmity with Him, and who bitterly hate Him.

Going back to the previous phrase, the pronoun "His" before "love" carries the weight of "His own." In other words, it is not in contrast with human love, but rather a type of love so set apart from man's understanding of such that there is no comparison.

When we look at this divine love displayed in the atonement, we have to ask ourselves how this is consistent with the divine wrath against sin. The same love that gave such respecting Calvary is equally opposed to sin; however, the ideas are not irreconcilable.

The answer is that God not only portrayed such great love by the act of Calvary but, at the same time, displayed His righteous anger and wrath against sin. He did it by pouring out His wrath on His only Son instead of you and me. So, it is a twofold display.

SIN

God will not, should not, and, in fact, cannot in any capacity, not even in the slightest, overlook even the smallest manifestation of sin, much less the gross evil of man's fallen condition. The answer is that His wrath, which, of necessity, must be exhibited against sin, was poured out upon the person of His Son, the Lord Jesus Christ, even though He had never sinned. As we have stated, He became the voluntary sin offering by agreeing to take the punishment of the wrath of God, which was necessary to display, that is, if God was to retain His righteousness, which He had to do.

In fact, that is the story of Isaiah, Chapter 53. The prophet said, *"Surely He has borne our griefs, and carried our sorrows: yet we did esteem Him stricken, smitten of God, and afflicted."*

He went on to say, *"But He was wounded for our transgressions, He was bruised for our iniquities: the chastisement of our peace was upon Him; and with His stripes we are healed."*

As well, this did not pertain to only a part of the human race, with the prophet further adding, *"All we like sheep have gone astray; we have turned every one to his own way; and the Lord has laid on Him the iniquity of us all"* (Isa. 53:4-6).

MUCH MORE THEN

"Much more then, being now justified by His blood, we shall be saved from wrath through Him" (Rom. 5:9).

The heading carries the idea that if Christ died for us while we were yet sinners (and He most definitely did), which means that we had no merit whatsoever, this should make us realize how much He will actually do for us now that we are redeemed. In effect, each born-again believer is a child of God, adopted, in fact, into the family (Rom. 8:31-34; Heb. 7:25).

Many believers have the problem of self-condemnation, which is so graphically outlined in Romans, Chapter 8. Struggling at times with sin and the flesh, Satan takes advantage of us by claiming that God's patience is about expended with us due to our many failures.

To be sure, in no way is this meant to condone sin, failure, or wrongdoing of any nature, but rather to express God's love to the believer. If He loved us so much while we were yet sinners, even that He would yet die for us while we were in that terrible state, how much more does He love us now that we are His? In no way will He ever lose patience with us and, thereby, cast us over, as Satan—the liar—suggests.

While the believer must never become complacent toward failure or weakness, at the same time, he must understand that as long as he places his trust in Christ and what Christ did for us at the Cross, God will never level condemnation at him. So, if, in fact, there is no condemnation, such is from the Evil One and not God.

In other words, the one pointing an accusing finger at the believer is the Devil and not the Lord. So, the believer must understand that and refuse to accept Satan's condemnation. He is to rest firmly in Christ, with the assurance that God always forgives and cleanses the supplicant believer (I Jn. 1:9) and guarantees ultimate victory.

BEING NOW JUSTIFIED BY HIS BLOOD

The heading tells us several wonderful things—so wonderful, in fact, that they are almost beyond comprehension.

First of all, we are now justified. That means that the believer is as fully justified now as he will be when he at long last stands before God in glorified form. There is no such thing as partial justification.

It also means that the new convert, in fact, even the one who gave his heart and life to Jesus just a few minutes ago, is as justified now as the greatest saint of God who has ever lived or ever will live.

As far as justification is concerned, it is a total, complete, and absolute finished work in the life of the believer, even immediately upon conversion. In other words, we don't work ourselves into justification. As we exhibit faith, it is automatically, totally, and completely given to us. While it is true that all the results of this work are not yet done and, in fact, will not be done until the resurrection of life, still, the *fact* of this work is done and completed.

It is this way because of the finished work of Christ. While the sinner believes Him and accepts what He did at Cavalry and the resurrection, the work is then done in totality. Were that work dependent upon us, to be sure, it would in no way be a finished work; however, it is not dependent on us, but rather Christ. So, in Him, it is done, finished, complete, absolute, total, and, as well, everlasting.

Sinners Jesus will receive;
Sound this word of grace to all
Who the heavenly pathway leave,
All who linger, all who fall.

Come, and He will give you rest;
Trust Him, for His Word is plain;
He will take the sinfulest;
Christ receives sinful men.

Now, my heart condemns me not
Pure before the law I stand;
He who cleansed me from all spot,
Satisfied its last demand.

Christ receives sinful men,
Even with all my sin;
Purged from every spot and stain,
Heaven with Him I enter in.

RIGHTEOUSNESS

As the reader surely knows by now, justification is a legal work carried out by God in the believing sinner's heart and life. In other words, upon faith in Christ, God declares the sinner to be clean, perfect, pure, without spot and without blemish, and as a consequence, everlastingly righteous because God can accept nothing else.

Once again, He declares that believing sinner in this fashion only after Christ. In other words, the pure, spotless, and absolute righteousness of God is freely given to the believing sinner. He then takes upon himself that spotless righteousness, while, at the same time, shedding the evil and the iniquity of his wickedness and sin.

This is all done by His blood, meaning that Jesus poured out His pure, untainted, and unstained life's blood at Calvary's Cross, which paid the price for man's redemption and satisfied heaven's just demands.

HEAVEN'S DEMANDS

So, what Jesus did at Calvary was far more to satisfy heaven's demands than anything that had to do with Satan or sin.

The way it affected Satan and sin was that Satan now had no more claim on the believing sinner once heaven's demands were satisfied. Before then, he could point an accusing finger at all of mankind and claim them as captives simply because they were stained and polluted by hellish sin, which Satan knew that God in no way could accept.

As the sin is automatically condemned by God, even as it must be, the sinner containing the sin is, at the same time, condemned. It is the same as a person having a contagious disease. Of necessity, that person must be quarantined, not because the person is hated, but because of his condition. It is the same way with sinners.

God did not and does not hate sinners, even as Romans 5:8 so loudly proclaims. In fact, He loves sinners; however, due to the fact that sinners carry a disease called sin, they must be quarantined in a place called hell. That is, unless they accept the atonement provided by God's own Son in the shedding of His precious blood at Calvary's Cross, and it has to be accepted before death.

WE SHALL BE SAVED FROM WRATH THROUGH HIM

The heading proclaims in stark clarity that the wrath of God is turned away from the sinner once faith is evidenced by the sinner toward Christ. As stated, God had to cleanse man from this deadly malady called sin, or else, the whole of humanity would be lost.

In the Greek text, the phrase actually says, "We shall be saved from *the* wrath through Him." This points out a particular wrath, which is the lake of fire—the manifestation of God's wrath against sin.

This is the reason that we have pointed several times to the fact that God does not so much condemn sinners simply because they are sinners, but rather because they refuse to accept His atonement for sin.

Consequently, in this one verse, we are guaranteed present peace and future safety. *"Now justified,"* assures the one, and *"we shall be saved,"* makes absolute the other.

THE ATONEMENT

Justification is based not upon the pious emotion or personal moral merit of a religious man, but upon the person of Christ and His atoning sacrifice. This divine foundation is displayed in the words, "His blood" and "through Him." Notice also the expression, *"Christ died,"* in Romans 5:8, set over against man's fourfold demerit—morally impotent (v. 6), ungodly (v. 6), sinful (v. 8), and hostile (v. 10).

Modern theology denies Christ's atonement and God's wrath. Both of these foundational truths of the gospel are here declared to be fundamental. Those who believe there is no wrath to fear naturally seek no Saviour and, so, cut themselves off from the salvation that is in Christ alone.

Christ's obedience unto death (Phil. 2:8), and that His death was a sin offering (I Cor. 15:3), is the central truth of this gospel. The effort to rid humanity of this foundational truth, to minimize it, or to substitute something for the incarnation is one of the saddest features of what is proudly termed "modern thought."

The expiatory sacrifice of Christ is the one and only eternal ground on which God can act in declaring ungodly men righteous.

Galatians 3:21 and many similar divine declarations reveal the hopelessness of standing before God in a righteousness that He will not accept. God will not accept a righteousness that is based upon any other principle than that of faith in the crucified Sin-Bearer, namely Christ.

CHRIST THE LAW KEEPER

Christ's perfect obedience to the law of God formed His own righteousness and gave virtue to His sacrifice, for a sacrifice for sin must have neither spot nor blemish. However, it was not the spotlessness of the lamb that made the atonement, but its poured-out blood—its surrendered life—for the blood is the life. With the judgment pronounced upon sin being death, that claim could only be vindicated and discharged by the suffering of death. Christ suffered that penalty and, in consequence, saved the believer from it.

FAITH BRINGS MAN CHRIST'S PERFECTION

If Christ's perfect obedience and perfect life alone would redeem man, then there was no need for Jesus to die. However, His incarnation, His virgin birth, His spotless life, and His healings and miracles could not redeem man, for as important as they were, they did not pay the price, for such could not pay the price.

Williams says, "But the Scripture declares that He died for sinners, so that it is His death that provides a spotless righteousness for sinners who believe in Him; and it was His obedience in life which gave the power to His suffering and death."

Christ never sinned one single time, not in word, thought, or deed. In fact, the perfect obedience of Christ in life and living was necessary in order for such perfection to be given to us upon believing faith. This transferred the believing sinner from lawbreaker to law keeper.

Then Christ addressed the broken law by giving Himself as a sacrifice on Calvary's Cross.

In fact, both were necessary—His perfect life and His perfect death.

ROMANS, THE ABCS OF THE GOSPEL

An intelligent grasp of this teaching is necessary for a knowledge of the gospel—the principle on which God can declare guilty men righteous. All of this that Paul proclaims sets out Christ's work for the believing sinner; however, it is not necessary at all for the sinner to understand all the rudiments of what is explained here. If it was necessary, no sinner would be saved because no sinner understands anything of the gospel, much less all that Christ did for the sinner.

So, all that is necessary for the sinner to be saved is for him to simply believe that Jesus is the Son of God and that He died for sinners. Believing that instantly transforms the sinner with all of his unrighteousness into a believer cloaked in the righteousness of God. That is the reason John 3:16 is so important. The sinner only has to *believe*.

However, having said that, it is imperative for the sinner, once he has become a believer, to set out to learn and understand the great rudiments of the gospel here laid out by the Holy Spirit through Paul. He should take it upon himself to learn and understand (which the Holy Spirit will grandly help him do) all that Jesus has done for us, at least as far as a poor human can understand such. To fail in that is to fail in victory.

WHY DID GOD DEMAND THE BLOOD OF JESUS AS PAYMENT OR ATONEMENT FOR SIN?

We have learned very graphically and succinctly of how Jesus shed His life's blood for the sin of man and of the necessity that it should be done, but why was this the price demanded by God?

When reading the Bible, we find that blood, which is *dam* in Hebrew and *haima* in Greek, is theologically significant in both testaments. In both, this word is linked with life and death. In both, blood introduces us to the depths of God's love for us and to His unique forgiveness.

OLD TESTAMENT

The word *dam* in the Old Testament occurs about 360 times. It is found most often in the Pentateuch and in Ezekiel.

The word *blood* is used generally in one of two ways:

1. It often indicates violence—the shedding of blood in war or murder—with the usual outcome being death.
2. In other instances, it is associated with the shedding of blood done in making a sacrifice to the Lord. Three Old Testament passages show the respect for life that God demanded from human beings, and they show the significance of blood.

GENESIS

At the very outset of time, the Lord said, *"Whoso sheds man's blood, by man shall his blood be shed"* (Gen. 9:6). In context, the blood of every living creature must be accounted for because that fluid is lifeblood. To shed the blood is to take the life, and although life is precious, the life of human beings made in God's image is uniquely precious (Gen. 9:4-6).

In fact, this is the reason for the demand for capital punishment for capital crimes. It is not to deter crime but to show how precious that life really is respecting the image of God.

Consequently, when a person takes the life of another in cold blood, he is showing disdain for the image of God, and the Word of God declares that the murderer must forfeit his own life.

LEVITICUS

"The life of the flesh (a creature) *is in the blood: and I have given it to you upon the altar to make an atonement for your souls* (I have given it to you to make atonement for yourselves on the altar)*"* (Lev. 17:11).

In Old Testament sacrifices, the blood of the sacrificial animal was drained, then sprinkled on the altar or ground, and the lifeless body was burned. The blood represented life. Blood sustains mortal life and may be offered to God in place of the sinner's life, which it was in Christ Jesus with His death on the Cross.

DEUTERONOMY

"Be sure that you eat not the blood (Be sure you do not eat the blood)*: for* (because) *the blood is the life; and you may* (must) *not eat the life with the flesh* (meat)*"* (Deut. 12:23).

Blood is neither to be drunk nor eaten with meat (Gen. 9:4). Blood is sacred fluid: Once it was taken from an animal, its sole use was for the sacrifice. Through this, the Old Testament saint was assured of the forgiveness of his sins because it pointed to the one who was coming, namely the Lord Jesus Christ.

In fact, the Holy Spirit reinforced this command, even under the new covenant, in the statement given by James at the great counsel in Jerusalem, recorded in Acts, Chapter 15. He said, pertaining to the new covenant believers, *"That you abstain from meats offered to idols, and from blood, and from things strangled, and from fornication"* (Acts 15:29).

This shows us how much this all-important truth was inculcated into the very spirit of Israel. They knew and understood the meaning of the offering of the animal sacrifices and what the shedding of their blood actually meant. As solemn and somber as this ceremony was, they knew beyond the shadow of a doubt what it represented. Understanding perfectly the promise given by God in the garden of Eden concerning the coming Redeemer (Gen. 3:15), they well understood that the sacrifices were only a substitute until the reality came, who would be Christ.

THE PROPHET

Above that, the prophets reinforced this over and over again, especially the prophet Isaiah in the giving of his great Chapter 53. This left absolutely no doubt as to that which the Redeemer would do.

So, they knew and understood perfectly well the preciousness of the blood and why it was precious. Consequently, this is what made their crucifixion of Christ so awful. Their denying and crucifying their Redeemer, in fact, the Redeemer of the world, was the most horrendous act in human history, and that is because of who it was that they crucified. There is no way that one could adequately describe the horror of what they did and the suffering they have endured because of this one act.

While it was necessary that Christ die and that He would die on the Cross, at least if man was to be redeemed, still, it was not at all ordained that Israel, God's chosen people, would do this horrible thing. With God being God, He could have effected the crucifixion in many and varied ways without His own people carrying out this dastardly act. His death was absolutely necessary, even as we are explaining here, but that Israel did this thing was totally and completely of their own doing, despite the pleas of Christ otherwise.

THE NEW TESTAMENT

The word *blood*—in the Greek *haima*—occurs 99 times in the New Testament. Often it refers to human bloodshed, representing violence and death, even as in the Old Testament.

Five times the New Testament speaks of "flesh and blood," to indicate human limitations and weakness. Blood is used in the book of Revelation to express the terrors of these days of judgment and is found 14 times in references to Old Testament sacrifices.

In reference to the blood of Christ, the word is used 38 times.

THE BLOOD OF OUR LORD AND
SAVIOUR JESUS CHRIST

When the blood of Christ is mentioned, it is always in reference either to the institution of the new covenant or to Jesus' death as a sacrifice of atonement.

Covenant plays a central role in the theology of the Old Testament. A covenant is an agreement or contract. The Old Testament covenants entered into by God took on the character of an oath or promise, for in them God bound Himself to do certain things for His people. He also told individuals how they could experience the benefits promised.

There were a number of ways to make a covenant in Old Testament times, but the most binding was a covenant instituted and sealed by blood (Gen. 15:8-21).

In the Old Testament, God promised that one day He would make a new covenant with His people. Under the new covenant, God promised to provide forgiveness and a new heart (inner transformation) (Jer. 31:33-34).

The death of Jesus (more specifically, the blood that He shed on Calvary) instituted this new covenant. Christ's blood sets the seal of God's promise on His offer of forgiveness through faith in the Son (Heb. 9:15-28).

THE LORD'S SUPPER

We meet the new covenant again in the cup of Communion (Mat. 26:28; Mk. 14:24; Lk. 22:20; I Cor. 11:25-27). We are told to drink the symbolic juice, recognizing the blood of Jesus as a sign of our participation in the blood of Christ (I Cor. 10:16).

This language reflects Jesus' discourse on the Bread of Life where He urged His hearers to *"drink"* His blood (Jn. 6:53-56).

The metaphor, for that's what it was, which was so startling to His audience, calls for appropriating by faith the sacrifice by which Jesus instituted the new covenant, while Communion affirms our faith in that sacrifice.

Consequently, as should be obvious, Jesus was not meaning for people to literally drink His blood, and neither does the grape juice turn into His literal blood in the Communion as claimed by Catholics and others. As stated, Christ was using a metaphor in both cases.

THE SACRIFICE OF CHRIST

Most references to the blood of Christ are linked directly with Calvary and recall the Old Testament link between blood and sacrifice. Thus, Romans 3:25, says that Christ's blood is the blood of atonement. Jesus offered Himself as a sacrifice for our sins.

The emphasis in many New Testament references is laid on the benefits won for us by Jesus' blood. It is by the blood of Christ that we are justified, which we are here studying (Rom. 5:9).

Through the blood of Christ, we have redemption (Eph. 1:7; Heb. 9:12) and have been delivered from our old, empty way of life (I Pet. 1:9). Jesus' blood has brought us near to God in the most intimate of relationships (Eph. 2:13), and has made peace for us by bringing us into harmony with our Lord (Col. 1:20).

Likewise, the blood of Christ has been effective in doing away with sin (Heb. 9:24-26). This involves forgiveness (Eph. 1:7), continual cleansing (I Jn. 1:7), and freedom from sin's binding power so that we can actively serve God with a cleansed conscience (Heb. 9:14; Rev. 1:5).

THE MEANING OF THE SACRIFICE

Against the background of the Old Testament, we come to understand the meaning of the sacrifice of Jesus on Calvary; however, it is through the teaching of the New Testament that we grasp the wonderful benefits purchased for us by the shed blood of our Lord.

The wages of sin was and is death. Consequently, when man fell, he was poisoned totally and completely—spirit, soul, and body. This meant that his life's flow of blood was contaminated, and now contained death instead of life.

To assuage this or to nullify its binding result of death, a perfect life had to be offered up. However, there was no perfect life in that all who were in Adam were judged as fallen creatures, unable to provide a sacrifice.

Consequently, God became man—the last Adam—and in so doing was born of the Virgin Mary. Therefore, He was not tainted as all of humanity otherwise was. He would pour out His perfect, unpolluted, untainted, and unstained, precious blood as an offering for sin, which heaven would accept.

In fact, perfect shed blood was the only thing that could be accepted because the life was in the blood.

Hallelujah, what a thought!
Jesus full salvation brought,
Victory, victory!
Let the powers of sin assail,
Heaven's grace can never fail,
Victory, yes, victory!

I am trusting in the Lord,
I am standing on His Word,
Victory, victory!
I have peace and joy within,
Since my life is free from sin,
Victory, yes, victory!

Shout your freedom everywhere,
His eternal peace declare,
Victory, victory!
Let us sing it here below,
In the face of every foe,
Victory, yes, victory!

We will sing it on that shore,
When this fleeting life is over,
Victory, victory!
Sing it here you ransomed throng,
Start the everlasting song:
Victory, yes victory!

Victory, yes, victory,
Hallelujah! I am free
Jesus gives me victory,
Glory, glory! Hallelujah!
He is all in all to me.

CHAPTER 3

RECONCILIATION

RECONCILIATION

"FOR IF, WHEN WE WERE ENEMIES, we were reconciled to God by the death of His Son, much more, being reconciled, we shall be saved by His life" (Rom. 5:10).

RECONCILIATION

The heading speaks of man being reconciled to God and not God being reconciled to man, which is unscriptural.

God doesn't need to be reconciled to man, at least in the sense in which we think, especially considering that He loves sinners. He loves them so much, in fact, that He gave His only begotten Son in order to save sinners. God reconciles men to Himself by changing their hearts and converting them from sin by the manifestation of His love in Christ.

Pulpit said, "This reconciliation is spoken of as effected once for all, for all mankind in the atonement, independently of and previously to, the conversion of sinners."

Once again this leads back to the statement of Paul that *"while we were yet sinners, Christ died for us"* (Rom. 5:8). In fact, this reconciliation is available to all of mankind and can be appropriated by faith to any sinner.

ENEMIES

As we have already stated, the word *enemies* applies only to man. In other words, man is the enemy of God, and God is not the enemy of man. Now, the truth is, man thinks of God as an enemy because the righteousness of God is always opposed to the sin of man. While it is certainly true that He is opposed to sin, He—in no stretch of the imagination—could be opposed to the sinner except in some limited situations.

Any parent is opposed to drugs or alcohol or any other vice that may tend to destroy the life of his child, at least if the parent is halfway sensible. So, because God is unalterably opposed to sin, even as He should be, that in no way makes Him an enemy.

REBELLION

Man is in a state of rebellion against God and not God against man. This rebellion has persisted since the fall, and it takes upon itself the personality of the reason for the fall.

At that time Adam and Eve—in a sense the representative parents of us all—stepped outside of the revealed will of God. They did it purposely, knowingly, and in direct violation of what God had said. Satan made them believe that God was withholding something good from them by demanding that they not eat of the Tree of Knowledge of Good and Evil.

So man carries that same thought with him presently and, in fact, always has. If he believes at all that there is a God, he imagines God as interfering with him, in effect, and not allowing him to have his full latitude. He has been deceived into thinking that what his soul and spirit crave can be fulfilled in the world. In other words, he believes the lie of Satan.

That is the reason that nothing can change man's attitude and spirit, with the exception of the proclamation of what Jesus did for man on Calvary's Cross, with the Holy Spirit bringing to bear His work of conviction on the human heart.

Wuest says, "Reconcile in the Greek is *katalasso* and means 'to change, exchange, to reconcile those of variance.' It means primarily 'to exchange and, hence, to change the relation of hostile parties into a relation of peace; to reconcile.'"

RECONCILIATION

This involves five things:

1. It begins with a movement of God toward man—to break down man's hostility, to commend God's love and holiness to him, and to convince him of the enormity and the consequence of his sin.
2. It is God who initiates this movement in the person and work of Jesus Christ, and He does it through the office and ministry of the Holy Spirit (Jn., Chpt., 16; Rom. 5:6, 8; II Cor. 5:18-19; Eph. 1:6; I Jn. 4:19).

3. For the reconciliation to be complete, a corresponding movement on man's part toward God must also be effected, as should be obvious. This speaks of man yielding to the appeal of Christ's self-sacrificing love, laying aside his enmity, renouncing his sin, and turning to God in faith and obedience.

4. As a result of man hearing and accepting the gospel, a consequent change of character results in man. This is brought about by the forgiving and cleansing of all sin, which brings about a thorough revolution in all of his dispositions and principles.

5. This change on man's part effects a change of relation on God's part as well. Sin, which rendered God hostile to man, has now been removed so that God can now receive man into fellowship and let loose upon him all of His fatherly love and grace (I Jn. 1:3, 7). Consequently, there is a complete reconciliation.

It must be understood that the only one who has to change is man. God does not have to change.

MUCH MORE, BEING RECONCILED, WE SHALL BE SAVED BY HIS LIFE

The heading speaks of the resurrection of Christ, whereas the previous phrase spoke of the crucifixion of Christ. Where the first had to do with one's salvation, the latter has to do with one's victorious walk in this life before God and man. This is found in Romans 6:4; however, it is speaking of resurrection life, but such cannot be had until one *"has been planted together in the likeness of His death"* (Rom. 6:5). It is the Cross that makes resurrection life possible, but only if we know and understand that great truth, realizing that we died with Christ, and now we are raised with Christ.

SANCTIFICATION

Paul was writing about justification in the first phrase; he is here writing about sanctification. Sanctification is a finished work of Christ, received by the believing sinner at conversion, which means "to be made clean and pure and to be set apart exclusively for the Lord." This must be done before the sinner can be justified, which actually all happens at once (I Cor. 6:11). Still, there is also a progressive sanctification that the Holy Spirit begins in the believer at the moment of conversion. It is impossible to declare one clean before one is made clean. Sanctification makes one clean, which takes place at conversion, while justification declares the work as a finished work.

STANDING

First of all, the new believer has a *standing* in Christ that never changes and is made possible by the work of sanctification, which is freely imputed and given at the moment of conversion. That standing never varies because it is anchored in Christ and based upon His perfect righteousness (I Cor. 6:11).

However, the *state* of our sanctification, as we begin to live for God, is something else altogether. Whereas the standing never varies, the state is constantly going up and down one might say. This fluctuation is pretty much according to our knowledge of the Word of God and our faith, or the lack of such, in appropriating what Christ has done for us in our own hearts and lives. This is what Paul is talking about here (I Thess. 5:23).

In our lives lived for God, Satan constantly attempts to foster upon us sins of the flesh. He will greatly succeed if we do not know our rightful place in Christ, which pertains to what Christ did at the Cross—our dying and being buried with Him, and then our being raised in *"newness of life"* (Rom. 6:4).

In other words, when Jesus came out of the tomb, He came out different than when He went in, now with a glorified body. He is victorious over all sin and every power of Satan. Consequently, we must understand, even as we will study more succinctly in Romans, Chapter 6, that all of this was done for us.

In other words, we were in Christ when He died and in Him when He was placed in the tomb (buried), which means that all of our sins were buried with Him. In addition, we were in Him when He was raised from the dead. Consequently, we are to follow Him so that He may live the resurrected life in us, which gives us victory over all the flesh and every attempt by Satan (Gal. 2:20-21). This is all done by faith and is carried out by the power of the Holy Spirit, even as Paul outlines in Romans, Chapter 8.

Once again, even as Romans 5:9 says, if God saved us when we were sinners—even upon the premise of our simple faith in Christ and what He did at Calvary—how much more will He give us victory in the flesh after we become His children?

SAVED BY HIS LIFE

I say these things because at times the struggle can be severe, with the believer wondering if victory is possible. But it is possible. In fact, it is not something that is to be done; it is something that has already been done in Christ. It is a matter of appropriating faith and understanding what Jesus really did for us, which we hope to open up more fully in commentary when we get to Romans, Chapter 6.

Incidentally, in Romans 5:10, the words, *"saved by His life,"* do not speak of His perfect example respecting the some 33 and one-half years in which He lived above all sin. That, within itself, could save no one, but it speaks rather of the pouring out of His life's blood at Calvary. While it is true that He wants us to have His perfect walk, still, the fact of that example cannot grant such to us in any capacity. The example only becomes real when we appropriate unto ourselves—by faith and by the power of the Holy Spirit—all that He did for us in His death, resurrection, and exaltation.

The world has ever attempted to emulate the life of Christ while ignoring what He did at Calvary, but such cannot be done. This is not a matter of mere ethics, but is actually of life and death—the life of Christ imparted to the sinner who is dead in trespasses and sins. All of that is anchored squarely in Calvary.

JOY

"And not only so, but we also joy in God through our Lord Jesus Christ, by whom we have now received the atonement" (Rom. 5:11).

The heading proclaims the fact that all sin has now been removed by our faith in Christ, and we have, thereby, been reconciled unto God. This should be the occasion of constant joy expressed at what the Lord has done for us. In fact, the believer is to *"glory* (boast)... *in the Cross of our Lord Jesus Christ"* (Gal. 6:14), which has made all of this possible. However, our trust in Christ is no false confidence and provides the only true joy that a human being can actually have.

THROUGH OUR LORD

All of this is through our Lord Jesus Christ, which, incidentally, is His resurrection name. We truly owe it all to Jesus.

It was effected totally and completely by what He did at the Cross. That's what makes the Cross so very important—actually the most important thing on the face of the earth, and for all time. Every single blessing that we receive from the Lord—every iota of relationship and everything, and I mean everything—is made possible by the Cross of Christ, referring to what Jesus there did.

While everything that our Lord did on this earth was of supreme significance, still, all pales in comparison to the Cross. As someone has said, and rightly so, "The Cross of Christ is the greatest display of God's wisdom that creation has ever known."

BY WHOM WE HAVE NOW
RECEIVED THE ATONEMENT

The heading takes us even further into the great plan of God. We have salvation now, even though we do not yet have all the results of salvation. The final results will come about at the resurrection of life of all believers, which is made possible by the crucifixion and the resurrection of Christ. At that time, every saint will be glorified, which will then complete the salvation process.

However, it must ever be understood that the Cross of Christ was never dependent on the resurrection. Actually, the resurrection was totally dependent on the Cross. In other words, if Jesus had failed to atone for even one sin, due to the fact that the wages of sin is death, then there could not have been a resurrection. The very fact of the resurrection tells us that the Lord accomplished everything at Calvary's Cross that was intended.

The word *atonement* here should have been translated "reconciliation" because that is what it actually means.

However, the word *atonement* not only means "to cover," but it also means "the making of two estranged parties as one," hence, reconciliation.

THE JOY OF THE LORD

Oppression by Satan can rob the believer of the joy that we should have, and I speak of joy 24 hours a day, seven days a week. It should be something that springs up from our innermost being, and that which actually never leaves, despite circumstances. That doesn't mean that the believer doesn't at times experience discouragement, etc., but it does mean that discouragement and oppression are never to rob him of his joy.

The Scripture plainly tells us: *"The joy of the Lord is your strength"* (Neh. 8:10).

This is an age that is filled with oppression, which often leads to depression. Such is probably the cause of more suicides than anything else.

Depression is like a pall that settles over a person. It's like 500 pounds is on his shoulders and all is dark, there is no light to be seen, and no way out. It's a feeling of helplessness and hopelessness, and it is never of God.

I cannot say that I know what depression is, for I don't recall that I've ever experienced such. I have most definitely experienced oppression.

The meaning of the word *oppression* is "an unjust or cruel exercise of authority or power, which comes from Satan." It can also be defined as "a sense of being weighed down in body or mind or both; it carries every earmark of depression and often leads to depression."

A PERSONAL EXPERIENCE

On a Sunday morning a short time ago at Family Worship Center, I was ministering on this very subject. All of a sudden, something dawned on me that had not come to mind in the recent past.

I realized that since the Lord began to open up the Message of the Cross to me, I had not experienced one moment of oppression from that time until the present, and it continues in that vein of victory. I personally feel that an understanding of the Cross of Christ is absolutely necessary as it regards victory over this terrible problem that afflicts so many.

Concerning oppression the Scripture says: *"How God anointed Jesus of Nazareth with the Holy Spirit and with power: who went about doing good, and healing all who were oppressed of the Devil"* (Acts 10:38).

What does it mean to understand the Cross of Christ?

Perhaps the following will help us to understand it to a greater degree:

- Jesus Christ is the source of everything we receive from God (Jn. 1:1-4; 14:6).

- Our Lord is the source; however, the Cross of Christ is the means, and the only means, by which all of these great blessings come to us (I Cor. 1:17-18; 2:2; Gal. 6:14).

- With Christ as the source and the Cross as the means, and the only means, Jesus Christ and Him crucified must ever be the object of our faith. This is of vital significance (Col. 2:10-15).

- With our Lord as the source and the Cross as the means, and with that being the object of our faith, then the Holy Spirit, who works exclusively within the parameters of the finished work of Christ, will grandly help us (Rom. 8:1-11).

Let's say that again because it is so very, very important: The Holy Spirit works exclusively within the parameters of the finished work of Christ. In other words, it is the Cross of Christ that gives the Holy Spirit the legal means to do all that He does.

Paul wrote, and I quote again: *"For the law of the Spirit of life in Christ Jesus has made me free from the law of sin and death"* (Rom. 8:2).

TOTAL VICTORY

It must ever be understood that Jesus Christ defeated the powers of darkness at Calvary's Cross. When I say defeated Satan and all of his cohorts, I mean totally and completely. Jesus atoned for all sin, and with sin being the means by which Satan causes great problems for every person, his ability to steal, kill, and destroy was taken away at Calvary.

THE CURSE OF THE BROKEN LAW

Paul also wrote saying: *"For as many as are of the works of the law are under the curse"* (Gal. 3:10).

Then he said, *"Christ has redeemed us from the curse of the law, being made a curse for us: for it is written, Cursed is every one who hangs on a tree"* (Gal. 3:13).

Paul also said, and I quote from The Expositor's Study Bible, including the notes:

> *And you are complete in Him* (the satisfaction of every spiritual want is found in Christ and made possible by the Cross), *which is the Head of all principality and power* (His headship

extends not only over the church, which voluntarily serves Him, but over all forces that are opposed to Him as well [Phil. 2:10-11])*:*

In whom also you are circumcised with the circumcision made without hands (that which is brought about by the Cross [Rom. 6:3-5]), *in putting off the body of the sins of the flesh by the circumcision of Christ* (refers to the old carnal nature that is defeated by the believer placing his faith totally in the Cross, which gives the Holy Spirit latitude to work):

Buried with Him in baptism (does not refer to water baptism, but rather to the believer baptized into the death of Christ, which refers to the crucifixion and Christ as our substitute [Rom. 6:3-4]), *wherein also you are risen with Him through the faith of the operation of God, who has raised Him from the dead.* (This does not refer to our future physical resurrection, but to that spiritual resurrection from a sinful state into divine life. We died with Him, we are buried with Him, and we rose with Him [Rom. 6:3-5], and herein lies the secret to all spiritual victory.)

And you, being dead in your sins and the uncircumcision of your flesh (speaks of spiritual death [i.e., 'separation from God'], which sin does!), *has He quickened together with Him* (refers to being made spiritually alive, which is done through being 'born again'), *having forgiven you all trespasses* (the Cross made it possible for all manner of sins to be forgiven and taken away);

Blotting out the handwriting of ordinances that was against us (pertains to the law of Moses, which was God's standard of righteousness that man could not reach), *which was contrary to us* (law is against us simply because we are unable to keep its precepts, no matter how hard we try), *and took it out of the way* (refers to the penalty of the law being removed), *nailing it to His Cross* (the law with its decrees was abolished in Christ's death as if crucified with Him, at least for all believers);

And having spoiled principalities and powers (Satan and all of his henchmen were defeated at the Cross by Christ atoning for all sin; sin was the legal right Satan had to hold man in captivity; with all sin atoned, he has no more legal right to hold anyone in bondage), *He* (Christ) *made a show of them openly* (what Jesus did at the Cross was in the face of the whole universe), *triumphing over them in it."* (The triumph is complete, and it was all done for us, meaning we can walk in power and perpetual victory due to the Cross.) (Col. 2:10-15).

No, the Bible does not teach sinless perfection, but it most definitely does teach that *"sin shall not have dominion over you"* (Rom. 6:14).

WHAT DOES DOMINION MEAN?

Dominion means that a person is dominated by an outside force, actually, demon spirits. This doesn't mean that such a believer is demon possessed, but it definitely does mean that such a person is demon *oppressed*. As we have stated, the Cross—and the Cross alone—is the answer for this. If every believer would place his faith exclusively in Christ and what Christ did at the Cross—and maintain it exclusively in Christ and what He did for us at the Cross—he would find that most problems would leave, especially oppression and suchlike. This is the answer for man's dilemma, and the only answer.

THE OFFENSE OF THE CROSS

The Cross, however, offends people, and I'll tell you why.

Paul said: *"And I, brethren, if I yet preach circumcision, why do I yet suffer persecution? then is the offense of the Cross ceased"* (Gal. 5:11).

How is the Cross an offense?

It is an offense to man, especially religious man, because it lays aside all of man's efforts of the flesh—that which a human being can do. It proclaims them to be worthless, and that doesn't sit well. We like to think that our religious activity affords us something. It really doesn't. The only source of victory—the only source of being what we ought to be in Christ—is by and through the Cross, which gives the Holy Spirit latitude to work within our lives and to bring about that which is needful and necessary.

What we are up against as believers is far beyond our personal strength. We must understand that. So, if we try to overcome by the means of the flesh, we will fail every single time.

So, that means that we must, by the help and grace of God, place our faith exclusively in Christ and the Cross. We must understand that it was there that every victory was won, that Satan was defeated in totality, and it was all done for you and me. Do you understand that? It was done *exclusively* for you and me. It only remains for us to take advantage of what the Lord has done, and to be sure, He has done everything that needs to be done, and it was done at the Cross.

It's hard for man to lay aside his own efforts and admit that they are worthless. In fact, our own efforts minister to our self-importance, and that makes us feel good. It's also the road to ruin.

Far too many believers accept the Cross of Christ as absolutely necessary for their salvation, but when it comes to their sanctification—how they live for God on a daily basis and how they grow in grace and the knowledge of the Lord—they have no idea whatsoever the great part that the Cross plays in all of this. Consequently, this means that most believers simply do not know how to live for God, and that includes the preachers. As someone has well said, "We were told *what* to do, but no one told us *how* to do it!"

The believer is to understand that every single thing that comes from God, all, and without fail, is made possible by what Jesus did at the Cross. Please understand that when we speak of the Cross, we aren't speaking of the wooden beam on which Jesus died, but rather what He there accomplished. What needs to be done, we cannot do it. We must have the help of the Holy Spirit, and to have that help, our faith must be exclusively in Christ and the Cross, even on a daily basis.

Jesus said, *"If any man will* (if you are going to) *come after Me, let him deny himself* (you must deny yourself), *and take up his* (the) *Cross daily, and follow Me"* (Lk. 9:23).

TO DENY YOURSELF

As stated, this does not refer to asceticism. It means that we are not to depend at all upon our personal strength, talent, education, motivation, etc. We are to look exclusively to Christ and what He did for us at the Cross. This then gives the Holy Spirit, who works exclusively within the framework of the finished work of Christ, the latitude to do what needs to be done. He will then greatly help us. This is God's way.

Paul wrote, *"The law of the Spirit of life in Christ Jesus has made me free from the law of sin and death"* (Rom. 8:2).

The word *atonement*, as given to us in Romans 5:11, would have been better translated (as previously stated) *reconciliation*. It could read, "By whom we have now been reconciled."

How can a sinful human being approach God? How do we deal with the sins and the failures that alienate us from Him? Please believe me when I say that these problems definitely do exist, not with one or two here and there, but, in reality, with all believers.

The Lord's solution to this basic problem is pictured in the atoning sacrifices of the Old Testament. Although sacrifices picture what became a reality in the death of Jesus at Calvary, a more proper understanding of this word opens up the greater reality of what the Lord has done for sinners in the realm of salvation.

First of all we must understand that sin is the problem. It cannot be overlooked, sidestepped, ignored, or above all, forgotten. It must be addressed. There was no way that man could address sin. He was a fallen creature, needing redemption. So, there is nothing that man could do that would address the problem, and I mean nothing. If there was to be recourse, it had to come from God. In other words, sin had to be atoned, and that refers to sin past, present, and future. That means sin of every description, including that which we would relate as insignificant and that which would be gross—all sin little and large.

Sin is the cause of all problems, all troubles, and all of man's inhumanity to his fellow man. As stated, sin is the problem.

In the final analysis, all sin is directed against God. It is the process of disobeying Him that has caused all the problems in the world.

ALL SIN IS A FORM OF INSANITY

Most people would not think of sin in the form of insanity, but that's what it is. It is contrary to all that is good, all that is right, and all that is holy. It steals, kills, and destroys (Jn. 10:10).

When Satan engineered the fall with Adam and Eve in the garden of Eden, which was done at the very dawn of time, the Evil One, no doubt, thought that he had won the day. Man was God's choice creation, even greater than the angels.

Now man was wrecked and ruined, and there was no way that he could redeem himself because in Adam's loins was every human being who would ever be born. Due to the fact that Adam had now fallen, this meant that everyone who was born thereafter would be fallen as well. So, Satan had it sewed up, or so he thought.

Angels could not redeem man simply because they were of another creation. As stated, man could not redeem himself due to his fallen nature. This would have presented to God a polluted sacrifice, which God could never accept.

So, how could man be redeemed?

The Lord, by and large, told Satan how it would be done, that is, if the Evil One understood what God had said. No doubt, he began to understand more and more as time went on, but I do not think that Satan fully understood the plan of God until it had been completed at Calvary's Cross.

The Lord said:

> *And I will put enmity* (animosity) *between you* (Satan) *and the woman* (presents the Lord now actually speaking to Satan, who had used the serpent; in effect, the Lord is saying to Satan, *'You used the woman to bring down the human race, and I will use the woman as an instrument to bring the Redeemer into the world, who will save the human race'*), *and between your seed* (mankind which follows Satan) *and her seed* (the Lord Jesus Christ); *it* (Christ) *shall bruise your head* (the victory that Jesus won at the Cross [Col. 2:10-15]), *and you shall bruise His heel* (the sufferings of the Cross) (Gen. 3:15) (The Expositor's Study Bible).

In this passage, we have the first mention of the Cross, although in veiled form.

THE INCARNATION

The incarnation is God becoming man, which He did.

Nearly 800 years before Christ, the great prophet Isaiah said, *"Therefore the Lord Himself shall give you a sign; Behold, a virgin shall conceive, and bear a Son, and shall call His name Immanuel"* (Isa. 7:14).

Without a doubt, this prophecy is one of the greatest, if not the greatest, in the Bible. In Hebrew, the word *virgin* is *haalmah*, which means *"the* virgin—the only one that ever was or ever will be a mother in this way."

The Son who would be born would be the Son of God.

The word *Immanuel* means "God with us." Such was fulfilled in Christ.

This prophecy was given by God as a rebuttal to the efforts of Satan working through the kings of Syria and Israel to unseat Ahaz. In other words, their efforts to make void the promise of God given to David would come to naught.

GOD BECOMING MAN

God would become man for many reasons, but the outright most important reason of all (and by far) was to go to the Cross. God, being Spirit, cannot die, so in order to die, which had to be if man was to be redeemed, God would have to become man, which He did. He did it for the sole purpose of atoning for all sin, which required a sacrifice that God could accept.

As previously stated, the terrible sin question would have to be addressed head on. It could not be sidestepped, it could not be ignored, and it could not be treated with disdain. The price had to be paid in full, that is, if God was to be true to His nature.

God can do anything. He is all-powerful, is all-knowing, and, as well, is everywhere. However, there are many, many things that God will not do because to do so would be in violation of His pure holiness, His perfect righteousness, and His perfect nature. To be true to His perfect nature, He would have to pay the full price in order for man to be redeemed.

Yes, He had the power to just speak the word and redemption would be effected, but, as stated, He would not do that because that would be treating sin lightly, and that He could not do.

SUBSTITUTION AND IDENTIFICATION

Jesus Christ would go to the Cross and offer up His perfect body as a perfect sacrifice, which He did. In the doing of this, He atoned for all sin—past, present, and future—at least for all who will believe (Jn. 3:16; Col. 2:10-15).

In effect, He became our substitute. He did for us what we could not do for ourselves.

All of us are fond of making the statement that we should have died on the Cross. However, it would have done us no good whatsoever had we done so. It would have presented, as stated, a polluted sacrifice to God, which He could not accept. No, only God could do this thing, and He did it through His Son and our Saviour, the Lord Jesus Christ.

To identify with Christ, all we have to do is simply evidence faith. When I speak of faith, I am meaning faith in Christ and what Christ did at the Cross for us.

If we leave off the Cross and have faith only in Christ, Paul labels such as *"another Jesus."*

He said:

> *But I fear, lest by any means, as the serpent beguiled Eve through his subtilty* (the strategy of Satan), *so your minds should be corrupted from the simplicity that is in Christ.* (The gospel of Christ is simple, but men complicate it by adding to the message.) *For if he who comes preaching another Jesus* (a Jesus who is not of the Cross), *whom we have not preached* (Paul's message was 'Jesus Christ and Him crucified'; anything else is 'another Jesus'), *or if you receive another spirit* (which is produced by preaching another Jesus), *which you have not received* (that's not what you received when we preached the true gospel to you), *or another gospel, which you have not accepted* (anything other than 'Jesus Christ and Him crucified' is 'another gospel'), *you might well bear with Him* (II Cor. 11:3-4) (The Expositor's Study Bible).

The Cross of Christ, where atonement was made, answered every question that man had or has, solved every problem, met every need, and opened the door for God to give us all the good things of heaven. In fact, Paul also tells us exactly what the gospel actually is.

He said, *"For Christ sent me not to baptize* (presents to us a cardinal truth), *but to preach the gospel* (the manner in which one may be saved from sin): *not with wisdom of words* (intellectualism is not the gospel), *lest the Cross of Christ should be made of none effect.* (This tells us in no uncertain terms that the Cross of Christ must always be the emphasis of the message.)" (I Cor. 1:17) (The Expositor's Study Bible).

Please understand that the Cross is big enough to contain the answer to every question, irrespective of what the question might be.

FAITH

The Lord does not require much of us, but He does require one thing and on that, He will not give ground.

He requires that we exhibit faith in Christ and what Christ did for us at the Cross, and to do so daily (Lk. 9:23).

IMPUTED RIGHTEOUSNESS

So, we evidence simple faith in Christ and what He did for us at the Cross, which means that we identify with Him in His death, burial, and resurrection. We are instantly given an imputed righteousness—the righteousness of God—which is a perfect righteousness. In fact, it is done instantly. This is the atonement.

Let us say it again: He alone is our substitute, ordained by God, and acceptable to God. In our identification with Him, and having faith in Him, we receive the benefit of His sacrifice, which frees us from all sin and removes the guilt. It is called justification by faith. However, in our identification with Him, even though it pertains to all He is and all He has done, more particularly, it points to Calvary and the resurrection. It is in that atoning work that we must be careful to identify with Him, for it was in that alone in which we were redeemed.

I am coming to Jesus for rest,
Rest, such as the purified know;
My soul is athirst to be blest,
To be washed and made whiter than snow.

In coming, my sin I deplore,
My weakness and poverty show;
I long to be saved evermore,
To be washed and made whiter than snow.

To Jesus I give up my all,
Every treasure and idol I know;
For His fullness of blessing I call,
Till His blood washes whiter than snow.

I am trusting in Jesus alone,
Trusting now His salvation to know;
And His blood does so fully atone,
I am washed and made whiter than snow.

My heart is in raptures of love,
Love, such as the ransomed ones know;
I am strengthened with might from above,
I am washed and made whiter than snow.

I believe Jesus saves,
And His blood washes whiter than snow,
I believe Jesus saves,
And His blood washes whiter than snow.

CHAPTER 4

SIN

SIN

"WHEREFORE, AS BY ONE MAN sin entered into the world, and death by sin; and so death passed upon all men, for that all have sinned" (Rom. 5:12).

BY ONE MAN SIN ENTERED INTO THE WORLD

The statement made in the heading narrows the facts as to the entrance of sin and death by one man, Adam. As well, this argument includes the introduction of life and sanctification by the second man, the Lord from heaven.

These two great federal heads of their respective sons are here contrasted, and the old and new natures are exhibited in opposition.

The argument of Romans 5:12 and later in verse 18 is that the one disobedience of the first man (Adam) assured death for all men, and the one obedience of the second man (Christ Jesus) secured life for all men, at least for all who will accept Him.

Williams said, "That is, all the sons of the first Adam by reason of their relationship to him and because they possess his sinful nature, stand in death, and all the sons of the last Adam in virtue of our relationship to Him, and because we possess His Spirit, stand in life."

The word *world* in the Greek is *kosmos* and means "the human race." It is the same word used in John 3:16—the world of sinners.

Sin originated with the angel Lucifer, who in rebelling against God, contracted a sinful nature. Adam in his disobedience was the channel through which sin entered the human race. Through sin, death entered the race physically and spiritually. The literal Greek which follows is, "And thus into all men death came throughout." That is, when death entered the race, it went throughout the race, affecting everyone.

Wuest said, "The reason why death affects all, Paul says, is that all sinned. Here Adam is looked upon as the federal head of the race, and that when he sinned, all of humanity sinned in him. It is Adam's initial sin that constituted him a sinner in which all human beings participated, and which brings death upon all. In other words, we are sinners, not necessarily because we have committed acts of sin, which we most definitely have, but because Adam sinned first of all."

THE MANNER OF CREATION

Every evidence is that when God created the angels, He created them all at the same time. Even though angels have different ranks as far as age is concerned, they are all the same; consequently, there has never been any baby angels.

So, when the angel Lucifer sinned (Isa. 14:12-15; Ezek. 28:11-19), his sin affected only himself. Even though a third of the angels threw in their lot with him, such was by their own volition, which made their sin even worse (Rev. 12:4).

As to whether the Lord made any attempt to redeem these fallen angels, the Scripture is silent.

HUMAN BEINGS AND PROCREATION

After bringing the world back to a habitable state (Gen., Chpt. 1), God then set about to create the human family (Gen. 1:26-27). However, He did this totally different than His creation of angels, in that He only made a pair of human beings—male and female—and gave them the power of procreation, i.e., to bring offspring into the world.

As an aside, the terrible sins of homosexuality and transgenderism are just that—terrible. They are probably the worst sins of all simply because they seek to change the order of God's creation.

No, homosexuals are not born that way any more than an alcoholic is born that way, or a gambler, etc. Admittedly, there are proclivities toward sin in various forms in every human being who is born. The answer for that, as it is with every human being in one way or another, is Jesus Christ, and only Jesus Christ.

At the same time, homosexuals, etc., should be treated with the same dignity and respect as any other human being.

True believers do not hate homosexuals, only the homosexuality. Likewise, true believers do not hate alcoholics, only the sin of alcoholism. While the Lord loves everybody—and I mean everybody—at the same time, He hates sin in any capacity.

The greatest text in the Word of God still is this: *"For God so loved the world, that He gave His only begotten Son, that whosoever believes in Him should not perish, but have everlasting life"* (Jn. 3:16).

Whereas the bringing of offspring into the world was a tremendous honor and privilege bestowed upon humanity, still, it imposed a great risk. The risk was that the seed of Adam carried with it not only the potential of great blessing and life but also of death. Whatever he did, be it positive or negative, would affect the entirety of the coming human race, irrespective of how many there would be. Whatever he was, the offspring would be.

In his original creation before the fall, Adam was destined to bring sons and daughters of God into the world. As stated, this was an honor of unprecedented proportions, even far above the angels (Lk. 3:38). In fact, every indication is that before the fall, Adam outranked the angels (Ps. 8).

Due to the fact that Adam was originally created in the image of God (Gen. 1:27), he also had the power to create even as God, which has passed down to his offspring. However, the difference between man and God is that Adam and his offspring can create things only out of that which already exists, while God can create something out of nothing.

There is no record in the Word of God that angels have the power to create anything, even though they are powerful creatures within themselves.

MAN

Observing man in his fallen state, it is not easy to grasp the fact that he was originally created higher even than the angels, but the evidence is that he was and will be again.

David wrote, *"What is man, that You are mindful of him? and the son of man, that you visit him? For You have made him a little lower than the angels (God), and have crowned him with glory and honor. You made him to have dominion over the works of Your hands; You have put all things under his feet"* (Ps. 8:4-6).

The word *angels* in Psalm 8:5 should have been translated "God" or "Godhead" because David used the Hebrew word *Elohim*, which means "God," and is so translated some 239 times elsewhere in the Old Testament.

However, when Adam fell from his lofty spiritual position that was given to him by God, he no longer had the ability or power to bring sons and daughters of God into the world. Now he could only bring forth sons and daughters *"in his own likeness, and after his image,"* and we continue to speak of Adam (Gen. 5:3). That speaks of the fallen state and original sin. In other words, every baby born thereafter, which has now numbered billions, was born with the awful poison of death because of original sin.

THE DEGREE OF THE FALL

Adam fell from total God-consciousness, which is bliss and security unparalleled in human thinking, down to the far,

far lower level of total self-consciousness. In other words, in the fall, man lost all consciousness of God.

It is very difficult for man, even redeemed man, to understand exactly how far that man has fallen due to the fact that it is impossible to relate to something of which there is no example.

There has been one example, and I speak of the Lord Jesus Christ. In Him—the last Adam—we observe total God-consciousness, but at the same time, we see the perfidy of the fallen race that murdered Him. In Him, we see what man was before the fall, and then we see the total depravity of man in murdering, in cold blood one might quickly add, the only good person who has ever lived. So much for man!

THE EFFECT ON MAN

Due to the fall, man is a perverted creature. The purpose of his being is to live and act entirely to the glory of his sovereign and beneficent Creator and to fulfill His will. In revolting against that purpose, he ceases to be truly man.

His true manhood consists in conformity to the image of God in which he was created. This image of God is manifested in man's original capacity for communion with his Creator; in his enjoyment exclusively of what is good; in his rationality that makes it possible for him alone of all creatures to hear and respond to the Word of God; in his knowledge of the truth and in the freedom which that knowledge ensures; and in government as the head of God's creation in obedience to the mandate to have dominion over every living thing and to subdue the earth.

THE IMAGE OF GOD

Yet, rebel as he will against the image of God with which he has been stamped, man cannot erase it because it is part of his very constitution as man.

It is evident, for example, in his pursuit of scientific knowledge, in his harnessing of the forces of nature, and in his development of culture, art, and civilization. However, at the same time, the efforts of fallen man are cursed with frustration.

This frustration is itself a proof of the perversity of the human heart. Thus, history shows that the very discoveries and advances that have promised the most good to mankind have, through misuse, brought great evils in their train. The man who does not love God does not love his fellow man. He is driven by selfish motives. The image of Satan, the great hater of God and man, is superimposed upon him. The result of the fall is that man now knows good and evil—a small amount of good, and much evil.

TRUTH

The spiritual and ethical effects of the fall are nowhere more graphically described than by Paul in Romans 1:18. All men, however ungodly and unrighteous they may be, know the truth about God and themselves, but they wickedly suppress this truth. It is, however, an inescapable truth, for the fact of the eternal power and Godhead of the Creator is manifested within them by their very constitution as God's creatures made in His image. That same eternal power and Godhead of the

Creator is also manifested all around them in the whole created order of the universe, which bears eloquent testimony to its origin as God's handiwork (Ps. 19:1).

DARKNESS RATHER THAN LIGHT

Therefore, man's state is not one of ignorance but of knowledge. His condemnation is that he loves darkness rather than light. His refusal to glorify God as God and his ingratitude lead him into intellectual vanity and futility.

Arrogantly professing himself to be wise, he, in fact, becomes a fool (Rom. 1:22). Having willfully cut himself adrift from the Creator in whom alone the meaning of his existence is to be found, he must seek that meaning elsewhere, for his creaturely finitude makes it impossible for him to cease from being a spiritual creature. His search becomes ever more foolish and degrading.

It carries him into the close irrationality of superstition and idolatry, into vileness and unnatural vice, and into all those evils—social and international—that give rise to the hatreds and miseries that disfigure our world.

The fall has, in brief, overthrown the true dignity of man (Rom. 1:23).

THE BIBLICAL DOCTRINE

It will be seen that the scriptural doctrine of the fall altogether contradicts the popular modern view of man as a being who, by a slow evolutionary development, has succeeded in rising from the primeval fear and groping ignorance of a humble origin to proud heights of religious sensitivity and insight. However, the Bible does not portray man as risen, but as fallen, and in the most desperate of situations.

It is only against this background that God's saving action in Christ takes on its proper significance. Through the grateful appropriation by faith of Christ's atoning work, which was forfeited by the fall, restored to man is: his true and intended dignity, the purpose of life, the image of God, and the way into the paradise of intimate communion with God. This takes place at the moment an individual is born again.

THE COMING OF CHRIST

Even though modern thought denies such, the New Testament proclaims the fall as a definite event in human history. It was an event, moreover, of such critical consequences for the whole human race that it stands side by side with, and explains, the other great crucial event of history, namely, the coming of Christ to save the world (Rom. 5:12; I Cor. 15:21).

Consequently, mankind, together with the rest of the created order, awaits a third and conclusive event of history, namely, the second advent of Christ at the end of this age. Then the effects of the fall will be finally abolished, unbelievers eternally judged, and the renewed creation—the new heavens and new earth wherein righteousness dwells—will be established in accordance with almighty God's immutable purposes (Acts 3:20; Rom. 8:19; II Pet. 3:13; Rev., Chpts. 21-22).

Thus, by God's grace, all that was lost in Adam, and much more than that, will be restored in Christ.

(The author is indebted to M.P. Williams, *The Ideas of the Fall and of Original Sin*; J.G. Machin, *The Christian View of Man*; and J. Murray, *The Imputation of Adam's Sin*.)

AND DEATH BY SIN

The heading first of all speaks of spiritual death, and by consequence, physical death.

When one reads these phrases, one is reading the cause of all of the suffering, sorrow, heartache, war, sickness, disease, and man's inhumanity to man, which characterizes the world, and has done so since the fall.

Sin is the problem! It is the problem not only for the world at large but, also, for the believer; however, there is a remedy, and that remedy is Jesus Christ and Him crucified. It took the Cross to address sin, to defeat sin, to eradicate sin, and to literally take it away (Jn. 1:29).

AND SO DEATH PASSED UPON ALL MEN, FOR THAT ALL HAVE SINNED

The heading consists of a two-pronged thrust.

The first prong consists of original sin. Inasmuch as the wages of sin is death, the dread malady of spiritual and physical death passes to every baby that is born. The well is poisoned, and it can only produce death.

Inasmuch as man is born in sin, this means that he has a depraved nature and, consequently, cannot live above sin, at least within himself.

Man keeps denying the fact of original sin and the depraved nature, claiming that proper education, environment, association, or even scientific research can alleviate the situation. However, the terrible sin problem remains, even as it must remain, at least as it responds to man's efforts.

The 20TH century is supposed to have been the most enlightened century of all the ages. To be sure, it has spawned the greatest scientific achievements in the annals of human history. Yet, the early 1940s witnessed the most horrifying spectacle of human history in the slaughter of some 6 million Jews by Hitler's henchmen.

The 1920s on up through the 1970s witnessed, as well, the deaths of untold millions more at the hands of Russian and Chinese communists. Each decade in this century, in fact, has brought a fresh horror, whether in Africa, Europe, or other parts of the world. So much for modern enlightenment!

JESUS CHRIST AND HIM CRUCIFIED

The Old Testament graphically outlines the horrors of sin, holding forth the atonement as the only answer. The New Testament, while agreeing with the old, at the same time, holds out an outstanding difference. All of the old terms and concepts of the Old Testament are brought over into the new—both deepened and strangely transformed. The one factor that makes this great difference is the work of Jesus Christ. He provides something that the saints of the Old Testament yearned for but could never find—real and certain victory over sin.

The doctrine of sin in the New Testament is dominated by the assurance that Christ has come to conquer that monster. Thus, whatever is said to emphasize sin's deadliness and serious-ness serves to magnify the greatness of the salvation from sin, which Christ has obtained.

As we should expect, each of the New Testament writers has a characteristic way of speaking about sin; however, Paul is, by all accounts, the most profound, but there is no essential disharmony amid the variety. Above all, they are all dominated by the assurance of Christ's effective answer to sin. That answer is the Cross of Christ.

As the first prong dealt with the fact of sin (original sin), the second prong deals with the nature of sin, which stems from the depraved nature, and guarantees that man will sin. So, man is shot down in two ways: he is a sinner by birth and a sinner by choice.

FOR UNTIL THE LAW SIN WAS IN THE WORLD

"For until the law sin was in the world: but sin is not imputed when there is no law" (Rom. 5:13).

The heading pictures Paul now proceeding to explain what he has said about all having sinned.

First of all, he is speaking of the law of Moses, which is obvious. This law properly exposed sin and defined it, which, of course, law is supposed to do.

From the time of Adam unto Moses was a period of about 2,400 years. During this time, there was no law given by God regarding sin. In other words, due to the lack of law, sin was not exposed or defined. Nevertheless, the absence of the law did not mean that sin was absent. In fact, it was in the world just as much as ever and was so bad, in fact, that the Lord was forced to drown the entirety of mankind during the flood, with the exception of one family—that of Noah. In other words, sin had become so absolutely awful that the Lord had to perform major surgery on the earth, or else the entirety of the creation would be lost, which it almost was anyway.

BUT SIN IS NOT IMPUTED WHEN THERE IS NO LAW

The heading simply means that those living between Adam and Moses had no sins charged to their account by reason of the nonexistence of the written law; however, that in no way meant they were not sinners and would not reap the result of their sin. It just meant that God did not reckon to their account each individual sin (Rev. 20:12).

NEVERTHELESS DEATH REIGNED FROM ADAM TO MOSES

"Nevertheless death reigned from Adam to Moses, even over them who had not sinned after the similitude of Adam's transgression, who is the figure of him who was to come" (Rom. 5:14).

The heading proclaims the fact that even though individual sins were not reckoned to the account of each person because the law had not yet been given, still, each person ultimately died, which proved the fact of their sins. Logic leads us to conclude that their deaths came by reason of Adam's sin and that they sinned in him—their federal head.

Even then the human body was so wondrously created and made by God that it took well over a thousand years for man to die. In other words, Chapter 5 of Genesis is not just a fable. It is the Word of God, meaning that these men lived as long as the Bible said they did.

By the time of Abraham, the life span had decreased drastically, with Abraham dying at 175 years old. His grandson, Jacob, died at 130. Joseph died at 120. By the time of David, which was 1,000 years before Christ, the life span had decreased again, with David dying at 70 years of age. When you look at the death rate around the world, it will average out at about 70 years.

All of this means that the human body, even though made of dust, was still so wondrously and miraculously created that it took that long for sin to wear it down.

EVEN OVER THEM WHO HAVE NOT SINNED AFTER THE SIMILITUDE OF ADAM'S TRANSGRESSION

The heading has reference to the fact that death did not come to these people by personal sin as it did in the case of Adam. Irrespective, they were just as guilty, even though they did not commit the same transgression that he did. In fact, their guilt was in his transgression, as is the guilt of all!

The subject is sin and its reproductive energy. One command was given to Adam. He disobeyed it. Many commands were given to Moses, and they were all disobeyed. So, the trespass abounded, i.e., the principle of evil that caused one trespass in Adam caused countless trespasses under law and so manifested sin's abounding fertility.

A fact of science illustrates the matter. A germ, when acted upon by a certain temperature, produces one deadly microbe, but with the temperature being raised, it produces millions.

Such was the moral effect that followed the introduction of law. The nature of the principle of evil—termed "sin"—and its venomous energy were made apparent to man's consciousness and to history.

WHO IS THE FIGURE OF
HIM WHO WAS TO COME

The heading speaks of Christ.

It is used in a doctrinal sense of a type—a person or thing prefiguring a future (Messianic) person or thing. In this sense, Adam is called a type of Jesus Christ, with each of the two having exercised a preeminent influence upon the human race: the former—Adam—that which is destructive, and the latter—Jesus—saving.

This is added so as to bring around the thought to the main subject of the chapter—the reconciliation of all mankind through Christ, at least those who will believe—to which the scriptural account of the condemnation of all mankind through Adam is given here. Adam is used as an analogy.

In Romans 5:14, *"Who"* refers to Adam, who has just been named for the first time, and *"Him who was to come,"* is Christ, who is called, in I Corinthians 15:45, *"The last Adam."* This means that there will never be another one because there will never be the need for another one.

As stated, Adam was a type of Christ, in that both represented all of humanity—one as the representative and author of the fallen, the other of restored humanity, with the transgression of the one and the obedience of the other alike affecting all (Rom. 5:18-19).

However, there is a vast difference between the two cases, and this is pointed out in Romans 5:15-17, which follow.

BUT NOT AS THE OFFENSE, SO ALSO IS THE FREE GIFT

"But not as the offense, so also is the free gift. For if through the offense of one many be dead, much more the grace of God, and the gift by grace, which is by one man, Jesus Christ, has abounded unto many" (Rom. 5:15).

The heading would have probably been better translated, *"As the offense, much more the free gift."* Paul is here drawing an analogy by drawing a contrast.

In other words, he is saying that Adam's offense touched the entirety of the world, and for all time, at least until Jesus rectified all things, but so did the grace of God in His free gift of salvation.

However, the idea is this: The grace of God was not merely on the same level as the offense, but it was of much greater proportion. That's what he meant by the phrase, *"But not as the offense."*

The word *offense* in the Greek is *paraptoma* and means "a falling alongside, a deviation from the right path."

Adam's original sin was the violation of the known will of God.

"Free gift" is the Greek word *charisma* and means "a gift of grace, a favor which one receives without merit of his own," referring here to the gift of eternal life in Christ Jesus.

The one transgression or offense of Adam resulted in the physical and spiritual death of all. However, as the fall of Adam caused great evil, the far greater work of the far greater Christ shall much more cause far greater results of good.

Yet, there is even a greater thrust in this statement: from a Christian point of view, the character of God is such that the comparison gives a much more certain basis of belief in what is gained through the last Adam than in the certainties of sin and death through the first Adam. In other words, much was lost in the fall, but that will be gained back, and even much more.

FOR IF THROUGH THE OFFENSE OF ONE MANY BE DEAD

The heading speaks of all who have died without God. Starting at the beginning and counting all the generations, this number would be in the billions. It speaks of spiritual death, which is separation from God, and is the most horrible thing that could ever happen to anyone. In effect, it speaks of the whole of humanity.

Spiritual death is a divine penalty and was brought about (as is obvious here) because of Adam's transgression. Romans 6:23 regards death as *"the wages of sin,"* i.e., as the due reward for sin. In addressing this, Paul spoke of certain sinners who knew God's decree but violated it anyway, with him adding that those who do such things deserve to die (Rom. 1:32).

SPIRITUAL DEATH

It is this thought of God's decree that underlies John's reference to the mortal sin (I Jn. 5:16). In essence, this speaks of blaspheming the Holy Spirit, which we will not now go into its many nuances; however, John's statement, plus many others in the Bible, present to us a very important truth. It enables us to see the full horror of spiritual death, which means "to be without God forever."

At the same time, these dire warnings give us hope. Men are not caught up in a web woven by blind fate so that, once having sinned, nothing can ever be done about it. God is over the whole process, and if He has decreed that death is the penalty for sin, which He has, He has also determined to give eternal life to sinful men, that is, if they will only take advantage of the atonement provided by Christ at Calvary.

To take such advantage, all that one has to do is express faith in Christ and what He did for us at the Cross. This will then cause God to impute to the believing sinner His perfect, spotless, righteousness. It is all done instantly upon faith, but it must be faith in the right object, which is Christ and Him crucified.

THE SECOND DEATH

Sometimes the New Testament emphasizes the serious consequences of sin by referring to *"the second death"* (Jude 1:12; Rev. 2:11). This expression signifies eternal perdition.

It is to be understood along with passages wherein our Lord spoke of *"everlasting fire, prepared for the Devil and his angels"* (Mat. 25:41), *"everlasting punishment* (set in contrast to 'eternal life')" (Mat. 25:46), and the like.

The final state of impenitent man is variously described as death, punishment, being lost, etc. Let me say it again: it is a state to be regarded with horror.

GOD, LOVE, AND DAMNATION

Many years ago, I preached a message entitled, "Can a Loving God Condemn a Soul to Eternal Hell, Burn Him There Forever and Forever, and Justify Himself in Doing So?"

It is quite a question!

Sometimes the objection is made that eternal hell (spiritual death) is inconsistent with the view of God as a loving God. However, such overlooks the fact that spiritual death is a state as well as an event. In other words, all who are without God are spiritually dead at this very moment, with the ultimate eternal conclusion being the lake of fire.

When we have grasped the truth that death is a state, we see the impossibility of the impenitent (those who refuse to repent) being saved. Salvation for such is a contradiction in terms. For salvation, a man must pass from death into life, which can only be done by the born-again experience that is brought about only through Jesus Christ and what He has done for us at the Cross (Jn. 5:24).

No! God gave His only Son, Jesus Christ, to serve as a sacrifice of death so that lost humanity might be saved. Considering that, God is not only just in condemning to eternal hell those who refuse such salvation, but contrary to modern thinking, He would be unjust in not doing so.

MUCH MORE THE GRACE OF GOD

The heading proclaims the inexhaustible power of this great attribute of grace.

If one man's trespass had such far-reaching effects, then how much more must the grace of God have far-reaching effects? God's grace must be more powerful than man's trespass, which it is! As well, it is not just somewhat more, but much more.

Grace is simply the goodness of God extended to undeserving people. In fact, there is no one in the world who deserves anything from God whatsoever as it regards that which is good; however, upon simple faith in Christ and what Christ has done for us at the Cross, God's grace is extended to us in an unlimited degree.

It is the Cross of Christ that makes the grace of God possible. God has no more grace now than He did before the Cross, but the Cross opened up the way that God could give man an unlimited degree of grace—upon simple, believing faith.

FOREKNOWLEDGE

Sometime in eternity past, it was determined by the Godhead that this universe and this planet called Earth would be created and would be populated by God's greatest creation— man. Through foreknowledge, God knew that man would fall. So, it was determined that God would become man in order to redeem man, which would be done by the means of the Cross. Being spirit, God cannot die. So, in order to die, the Creator would have to become a creation.

Then it was decided that God would deal with man by the means of grace. Grace has to be a choice, and if it's not, then it's not really grace.

Once grace was chosen by God as the means by which He would deal with mankind (and we speak of fallen man), then God had no choice but to extend mercy. Mercy is a normal outgrowth of grace. In fact, the mercy of God endures forever simply because grace endures forever. From day one, every human being who has ever been saved has been saved because of the grace of God. Not one single person ever earned anything from God, as it is impossible for anyone to earn anything from God.

AND THE GIFT BY GRACE

This short heading presents Jesus as that gift.

The one trespass of the one original transgressor did indeed render all mankind liable to condemnation; however, the free gift in Christ annulled the effect, not only of that one trespass but also of all subsequent trespasses of mankind. An immense debt accumulating through the ages of human history—in addition to the original debt—was obliterated by that one free grant.

However, we are not to gather from these statements that the Holy Spirit through Paul is speaking of a universal salvation to the extent that due to what Christ did, all are saved. The truth is that all *can* be saved, but the truth, also, is that all are not saved. In fact, most will not be saved, with only a few accepting eternal life, at least considering the whole of mankind (Mat. 7:13-14).

Irrespective, the fault is not God's but man's. The Lord has made salvation available to all, and while it is true that some have more opportunity than others, still, if anyone wants to come, he can (Rev. 22:17).

WHICH IS BY ONE MAN, JESUS CHRIST, HAS ABOUNDED UNTO MANY

The heading signifies that this one man, the Lord Jesus Christ, nullified the offense of the one man, Adam.

In fact, the original trespass introduced a temporary reign of death, while the free gift of righteousness introduced life in which the partakers of the gift themselves—triumphant over death—will live and reign forever in Christ.

As stated, this gift of grace has abounded unto many, and could, in effect, abound unto all, that is, if they will only believe.

However, it must be understood that this gift is by Jesus Christ. He is the one who paid the price at Calvary's Cross, which means that every debt of sin was canceled, at least for those who will believe. That's the reason that in order for one to be saved, one must accept the Lord Jesus Christ as one's Saviour and one's Lord. There is no salvation in any other. It is Jesus Christ we must accept simply because He is the one who paid the price at Calvary's Cross. No one else paid it because no one else could pay it. He paid it all; consequently, He is due the homage, love, and respect that any person will give if he truly knows Him.

The statement and the way is simple, *"Believe on the Lord Jesus Christ, and you shall be saved"* (Acts 16:31).

I wandered in the shades of night
Till Jesus came to me,
And with the sunlight of His love,
Bid all my darkness flee.

Though clouds may gather in the sky,
And billows round me roll,
However dark the world may be,
I've sunlight in my soul.

While walking in the light of God,
I sweet communion find;
I press with holy vigor on
And leave this world behind.

I cross the wide extended fields,
I journey over the plain,
And in the sunlight of His love
I reap the golden grain.

Soon I shall see Him as He is,
The light that came to me,
Behold the brightness of His face
Throughout eternity.

CHAPTER 5

THE GIFT

THE GIFT

"AND NOT AS IT WAS by one who sinned, so is the gift: for the judgment was by one to condemnation, but the free gift is of many offenses unto justification" (Rom. 5:16).

AND NOT AS IT WAS BY ONE WHO SINNED, SO IS THE GIFT

The heading presents the same thing as the first phrase of the last verse—Paul is once again drawing a contrast: one man, Adam, brought the transgression, which affected the entire race, while one man, Christ, brought eternal life, at least for all who will believe. However, there the similarity ends.

The contrast of eternal life, as given by Christ, up beside the offense of Adam, quickly becomes obvious.

Adam's one transgression affected all people, even though all the billions had not yet been born, and as a result, they could not have committed any sin. However, they were judged as sinners and, in fact, must be judged as sinners because all were in Adam.

By comparison, the free gift of salvation as purchased by Christ at Calvary was not for the unborn but for those who actually were sinners, in effect, having committed many trespasses. Irrespective, simple faith in Christ would wash clean all sin and cleanse from all unrighteousness.

FOR THE JUDGMENT WAS BY
ONE TO CONDEMNATION

The heading speaks of Adam failing God and then incurring the judgment of God, which was an absolute necessity. Perfect righteousness must condemn all sin in the flesh, for there is no alternative, as should be obvious. Consequently, the condemnation came upon all because, theoretically, all were in Adam's loins.

BUT THE FREE GIFT IS OF MANY
OFFENSES UNTO JUSTIFICATION

The heading verifies what we have said about the eternal life offered by Christ to believing sinners. As stated, this free gift cleanses from many offenses, in effect, all offenses, at least for all who will believe.

This free gift not only addresses itself to all offenses, but, as well, it effects a legal work that God can justly recognize and declare the sinner "not guilty." He can do such because of the sinner's faith in Christ, who (Christ) took the penalty for all these offenses, thereby, wiping the slate clean, at least for all who will believe. Once again, this is justification by faith, which is the bedrock of Paul's argument respecting the new covenant.

FOR IF BY ONE MAN'S OFFENSE
DEATH REIGNED BY ONE

"For if by one man's offense death reigned by one; much more they which receive abundance of grace and of the gift of righteousness shall reign in life by one, Jesus Christ" (Rom. 5:17).

The heading refers to Adam's failure, with the result being death; consequently, death reigns over all of mankind.

The word *reign* in the Greek is *basileuo* and means "to rule from a foundation of power." As a result, man, who is God's choicest creation, is little able to utilize his ability and energy, with death overtaking him even on short notice. In fact, man was not originally created to die, even though he was of flesh, even as the resurrected body will be of flesh. Still, it was flesh that was incorruptible and immortal. Corruption and mortality came after the fall.

MUCH MORE THEY WHICH RECEIVE
ABUNDANCE OF GRACE

The heading presents unlimited, unmerited favor. It is not just grace, but it is abundance of grace! All of this comes upon one exhibiting simple faith in Christ. The idea is that the grace is more, much more, than the debilitating effects of sin.

Unfortunately, the far greater majority of the modern church attempts to live for God by the means of law rather than grace. There are only two places for a person to be, and that goes for every human being on the face of the earth. It is law or grace.

Paul said, *"For sin shall not have dominion over you: for you are not under the law, but under grace"* (Rom. 6:14).

What did Paul mean by the statement, *"For you are not under the law, but under grace?"*

Under law, there was only the command not to do certain things, but there was no power to help the person obey. So, under law, the person was doomed to constant failure.

Grace is available to any and every person who puts his faith in Christ and what Christ did for us at the Cross. The Holy Spirit, who is God, and who has all power, will help us do what needs to be done. That's the difference in law and grace. The difference is great, to say the least.

While believers are not under law in any capacity, the truth is, all the host of unredeemed are under law, whether they understand that or not. In fact, most of them, if not all of them, would scoff at the idea that they are under the law; nevertheless, that's exactly where they are. To be sure, they have broken it repeatedly, even constantly. The penalty for that is death. Death refers to acute separation from God, which ultimately means eternal hell.

John wrote, *"For the law was given by Moses, but grace and truth came by Jesus Christ"* (Jn. 1:17).

There's only one way to escape the penalty of the law, which, as stated, is death, and that is by the acceptance of Jesus Christ as one's Saviour and Lord. Jesus kept the law perfectly on behalf of all who accept Him. Thereby, He transfers His perfection to the believing sinner, which is done upon faith.

As it regards the broken law, of which all are guilty, He gave Himself on the Cross of Calvary, which paid in full the just demands of the law. So, if one accepts Christ, one is released from the penalty of the law, but only if one fully accepts Christ as one's Saviour and Lord.

AND OF THE GIFT OF RIGHTEOUSNESS

The heading proclaims righteousness, in effect, God's righteousness, which speaks of the essence of perfect morality. As stated, it is a free gift. In fact, it must be a free gift if it is to be by grace.

The moment the believing sinner accepts Christ, and I mean that particular moment, God imputes to that believing sinner a spotless, pure, and incorruptible righteousness, in effect, the righteousness of God. It's the only righteousness that God will accept. Anything else is self-righteousness, which God can never accept.

The only way this perfect righteousness of God can be received by an individual is for his faith to be in Christ and what Christ has done for us at the Cross. It is the Cross, and the Cross alone, that opens the door for God to impute such righteousness. He will accept nothing else.

This is why the Cross of Christ is so very, very important. In fact, the Cross of Christ is the foundation of the entirety of the Word and work of God. On this foundation, every biblical doctrine is constructed. This is where false doctrine comes in. It is doctrine that does not have as its foundation the Cross of Christ.

Any attempt to live for God by means other than the Cross, and I mean any attempt, always concludes in self-righteousness, which, as stated, God can never accept. The further away the church gets from the Cross, the more self-righteous it becomes.

SHALL REIGN IN LIFE BY ONE, JESUS CHRIST

The heading proclaims the believer as reigning, even as death had once reigned, but from a position of much greater power than that of death. All is in Jesus Christ.

In this verse, death and life are contrasted. However, while it says that death reigned over man, it does not say that life reigns over the believer, for that would invest life with tyranny. It does say that the believer reigns in life, and, thus, the environment of freedom and liberty is preserved. This life is legally secured by the life and death of Christ.

If, in fact, life reigned over humanity, it would be the same as Adam and Eve eating of the Tree of Life after the fall and, thereby, living forever on earth in that fallen state. They would have continued to fall deeper and deeper into depravity without physical death bringing this hell to a halt. The results would have been unthinkable, which is the reason God drove them out of the garden (Gen. 3:22-24).

OBEDIENCE

Christ's one righteous act of obedience was His obedience unto death (Phil. 2:8), but this was the climax for His whole mission on earth, which was one great act of obedience. This doesn't mean that Christ learned to be obedient, for had that been the case, that would mean that He had been disobedient, which He never was. It simply means that He voluntarily gave Himself over to death, which was an absolute necessity if man was to be redeemed.

The many, therefore, who are born of Adam and, consequently, possess his sinful nature are hopelessly lost, for they cannot undo the fact of their birth. As well, the many who are born of the last Adam and, consequently, possess His nature, are absolutely saved as much, and even more, as those of Adam are absolutely lost. However, this salvation is afforded only to those who are in Christ Jesus.

VICTORY OVER DEATH

An interesting feature of New Testament teaching on death is that the emphasis is on life. If we look up a concordance, we find that in most places where the word *dead* is used, it is of resurrection from the dead or the like. The Scripture faces death as it faces all reality, but its interest is in life, and death is treated more or less incidentally as that from which men are saved.

Christ took upon Him our nature (the incarnation) *"that through death He might destroy him who had the power of death, that is, the Devil"* (Heb. 2:14).

CHRIST CAME TO PUT AN END TO DEATH

The Devil's power is always regarded as subject to God's over-ruling (Job 2:6; Lk. 12:5). He is no absolute disposer of death. Nevertheless, death, the negation of life, is his proper sphere.

Christ came to put an end to death. It was through death, as the passage in Hebrews indicates, that He defeated Satan. It was through death that He put away our sin. The death He died, He died to sin once for all (Rom. 6:10). Apart from Christ, death is the supreme enemy, the symbol of our alienation from God, and the ultimate horror, but Christ has used death to deliver men from death. In other words, He died that men may live.

It is significant that the New Testament can speak of believers as sleeping rather than as dying (I Thess. 4:14).

Jesus bore the full horror of death; therefore, for those who are in Christ, death has been transformed so that it is no more than sleep. Even then, it is the body alone that sleeps, with the soul and the spirit of the believer instantly going to be with Christ at the time of death.

THE RESURRECTION

The extent of the victory over death that Christ won is indicated by His resurrection. *"Knowing that Christ being raised from the dead ... death has no more dominion over Him"* (Rom. 6:9).

The resurrection is the great triumphal event, and the whole of the New Testament note of victory originates here.

Christ is the "Prince of life" (Acts 3:15); He is *"Lord both of the dead and living"* (Rom. 14:9); and He is *"the Word of Life"* (I Jn. 1:1).

His victory over death is complete, and His victory is made available to His people. Death's destruction is certain (I Cor. 15:26, 54; Rev. 21:4). The second death has no power over the believer (Rev. 2:11; 20:6).

In keeping with this, the New Testament understands eternal life not as the immortality of the soul, but in terms of the resurrection of the body. Nothing could more graphically illustrate the finality and the completeness of death's defeat.

A GLORIOUS PRESENT
AND A GLORIOUS FUTURE

Not only is there a glorious future for the believer, but there is also a glorious present. The believer has already passed out of death and into life (Jn. 5:24; I Jn. 3:14). He is *"free from the law of sin and death"* (Rom. 8:2), and that means free *now!* Death cannot separate him from God (Rom. 8:38). Jesus said, *"If a man keep My saying, he shall never see death"* (Jn. 8:51). Such words do not deny the reality of biological death. Rather, they point us to the truth that the death of Jesus means that the believer has passed altogether out of the state that is death.

He is brought into a new state, which is aptly characterized as life. He will, in due course, pass through the gateway we call death, but the sting has been drawn. The death and resurrection of Jesus means victory over death for His followers.

THEREFORE AS BY THE OFFENSE OF ONE JUDGMENT CAME UPON ALL MEN TO CONDEMNATION

"Therefore as by the offense of one judgment came upon all men to condemnation; even so by the righteousness of one the free gift came upon all men unto justification of life" (Rom. 5:18).

The heading proclaims Paul saying the same thing that he has already said several times, and he does so for purpose.

When the Holy Spirit repeats something of this nature, especially in as many ways as Paul has repeated it, among other things, He is proclaiming the significance of the event and that we should understand what is being said. As should be obvious, for man to know the reason for his present dilemma is necessary. If he does not know the dilemma and what caused such, at the same time, he, as well, will not know and understand the solution.

Once again, Paul states the cause of the terrible judgment that has come upon all men, even a judgment of condemnation. It came by the fall of the federal head—Adam.

EVEN SO BY THE RIGHTEOUSNESS OF ONE THE FREE GIFT CAME UPON ALL MEN UNTO JUSTIFICATION OF LIFE

The heading now proclaims the glorious solution.

Man had no righteousness and, in fact, could not obtain any righteousness, that is, the type which God would accept.

Therefore, the righteousness that is of one—Jesus Christ—is freely given to all who will simply believe. It is called justification of life.

This means that sinners are made righteous by simply believing Christ and are, thereby, declared as justified, which means "not guilty." Sin had brought death, but justification brings life.

FOR AS BY ONE MAN'S DISOBEDIENCE MANY WERE MADE SINNERS

"For as by one man's disobedience many were made sinners, so by the obedience of one shall many be made righteous" (Rom. 5:19).

The heading actually refers to all, at least all who will receive Christ, which are many.

The word *disobedience* in the Greek is *parakoe* and means "to mishear, or to disobey; neglect to hear." This is one of the nine words for *sin* in the New Testament.

It describes the nature of Adam's first act of sin—the one act that plunged the entire race into sin with its accompanying degradation and misery.

In a fuller sense, disobedience is "a failing to hear" or "hearing amiss." In other words, it is the notion of active disobedience that follows on this inattentive or careless hearing, being superinduced upon the word; or it may be the sin being regarded is already committed by the failing to listen when God is speaking. It need hardly be observed how continually in the Old Testament, disobedience is described as a refusal to hear (Jer. 11:10, 35:17), and it appears literally as such in Acts 7:57.

SO BY THE OBEDIENCE OF ONE SHALL MANY BE MADE RIGHTEOUS

The heading pertains to the obedience of Christ as opposed to the disobedience of Adam.

Though the doctrine of the atonement in all its depth is beyond our comprehension, yet, it is important for us to observe the various aspects in which it is presented to us in Scripture. Here, the idea suggested is that of Christ, as the representative of humanity, satisfying divine righteousness by perfect obedience to the divine will and, thus, offering to God for man what man had lost the power of offering. To do this, Jesus had to become *"obedient unto death, even the death of the Cross"* (Phil. 2:8).

The word *obedience* in the Greek is *hupakoe* and means "to hear," literally, "to hear under." The idea is that of a willing listening to authority. Thayer defines it as "obedience, compliance, submission."

By the one act of Adam in disobeying God, the human race was constituted sinful, and this by the judicial act of God. Likewise, by the one act of obedience of the Lord Jesus, all who believe are constituted righteous, and this also by the judicial act of God.

The word *made*, as it refers to *righteous,* in the Greek is *poieo* and refers to a "mechanical operation such as that of making a spear out of wood and iron." It refers to the act of changing a certain material object so as to fit it for a certain purpose.

SALVATION MORE THAN A MERE PHILOSOPHY

This is the reason that salvation is far more than mere philosophy. In fact, the sinner must be made new, in effect, a *"new creature* (creation)*"* (II Cor. 5:17).

This completely shoots down the psychological approach of rehabilitation—a word not even found in the Bible. Rehabilitation, as stated, stems from humanistic psychology, which claims "to restore to a former capacity" or "to restore to a condition of health or useful and constructive activity."

The thought is good, but the actual results are zero.

First of all, how can anyone be *re*habilitated who has never been habilitated? Psychology starts from the erroneous premise that all men are good, and if they go bad, it is because of external forces, etc. So, they attempt to expose these external forces (whatever they may be), isolate them, and bring the individual around these things, hopefully, to a position of health.

THE BIBLE

The Bible teaches the very opposite in that man is inherently bad, and it's all due to the fact of Adam's fall (Rom., Chpts. 1-3). Consequently, bad is all he can do, or worse! Understanding that, there is nothing to which man can be rehabilitated.

So, the Holy Spirit through Christ starts out on an entirely different premise, with the object in view of making a completely new creation out of the sinner. In other words, He has to *make* righteousness for the sinner, which He will do, and will freely impute such to him upon simple faith in Christ (Jn. 3:16). Such righteousness is made by virtue of the Cross.

Surely it should be overly obvious as to the simplicity of the gospel (as given here by Paul) so that no one need misunderstand. In view of that, how can preachers who call themselves saved and even Spirit-filled, fall for the lie of psychology, which is so obviously contradictory to the gospel?

The work that man desperately needs, which is to be made a new person in Christ (and can only be done in Christ), is not in the power of man to bring about. In fact, it is literally impossible. Common spiritual sense tells one that if such were possible, Jesus would not have had to come to this sinful world and pay the terrible price He paid for the redemption of humanity. That should go without saying! And yet, almost the entirety of the church, even the Pentecostal varieties whose very claim once was the power of God, has bought into this lie.

I have asked why, and I think the truth is that these preachers, whomever they may be, simply do not believe God anymore. They claim to do so, but their actions speak otherwise!

THE CROSS OF CHRIST

The only answer for man's dilemma, and I mean the only answer, is the Cross of Christ—what Jesus there did. Now it comes down to the question: Do we believe what our Lord did at the Cross or not? At the Cross, Jesus atoned for all sin—past, present, and future—at least for all who will believe (Jn. 3:16; Col. 2:10-15; Rom. 6:3-14).

One of the major problems in the church, and perhaps always has been, is ignorance of what the Bible actually teaches. In other words, most every believer understands the Cross, at least to a degree, as it regards salvation. "Jesus died for me," is perhaps the greatest statement that anyone could ever make; however, that's as far as it goes for most.

Sanctification speaks of how we live this life, how we grow in grace and the knowledge of the Lord, and how we have victory over the world, the flesh, and the Devil. This is all made possible by the Cross of Christ, and only by the Cross of Christ. The great question is, do we believe that?

It is understandable why the world does not believe what I've just stated, but it is not at all understandable why the church doesn't believe it. The truth is, the church doesn't believe it.

One cannot have both psychology and the Cross of Christ. Either one cancels out the other. One has to go. Tragically, the Cross of Christ is that which has been thrown aside as it regards the modern church. It has opted for humanistic psychology, hook, line, and sinker. To be sure, there is no help in psychology, no cure in psychology, and no healing in psychology. In fact, there is nothing in psychology. It is built on a lie and has or knows no truth.

MOREOVER THE LAW ENTERED, THAT THE OFFENSE MIGHT ABOUND

"Moreover the law entered, that the offence might abound. But where sin abounded, grace did much more abound" (Rom. 5:20).

The law, as given in this verse, has reference to the law of Moses. As it has already been stated, sin was active and real before the law, but because there was no law, it was not imputed as offenses by the perpetrators. Nevertheless, they were still sinners and died lost.

However, when the law of Moses was given, which was about 2,400 years after Adam, its very purpose was to expose sin and define it. When it did this, offenses abounded, as would be obvious.

Wuest says, "The offense is multiplied because the law encountering the flesh, evokes its natural antagonism to God (antagonism of the flesh to God), and so stimulates it into disobedience. As the offense multiplied, and for several reasons, the need of redemption, and the sense of that need were intensified."

Wuest went on to say, "Not primarily of the greater consciousness and acknowledgment, but the increase of actual transgressions."

Why did law cause sin to abound? First of all, law always has that effect, even the law of God. That is not to be misunderstood as to think that the law of God was unholy or unrighteous. Actually, it was the very opposite! The things that God demanded of Israel were right and proper and what man ought to do everywhere.

THE TEN COMMANDMENTS

As we have stated previously, even though the law had many peripheral commands and statutes, still, the central core always was the Ten Commandments. As spokes on a wheel, everything led to that hub.

However, as simple as the Ten Commandments were, Israel still could not obey them, at least not in her own power, and neither can man presently. He is lacking in capability of doing such, no matter how hard he tries. This is because of the depraved nature of man due to the fall, which Paul is addressing here.

In setting out to keep these laws, man always failed. Actually, the harder he tried, the more he failed! The reason points to *"the law of sin and death"* in his flesh (Rom. 8:2).

As well, the very presence of law created a desire to do the opposite of what the law demanded. That again is the law of sin and death, which, as should be obvious, is not the law of Moses.

LAW OF ANY NATURE

It should be quickly added that the very moment the modern Christian or church institutes law of any nature, it will have the same effect upon the believer as the old law of Moses. Instead of bringing about holiness and righteousness, as some think, the efforts to keep such do the very opposite—increases failure. The reason is obvious.

That is what law is designed to do. And yet, I think that every single Christian at one time or another has attempted to bring about righteousness by means of some type of law, whether originated of himself or his church. Such may sound good to the religious mind, but it will bode ill every time.

It should be quickly added that anything and everything that's not the Cross is law. We must understand that religious law is the greatest culprit of all, and because it is religious, this makes us think that it is satisfactory and helpful. It isn't. Law in any capacity is unworkable. Law and grace cannot function in the same capacity. One or the other must go. Grace comes by the Cross, while law comes by man.

Actually, one of the designs of the law was that Israel would see that it was impossible of obedience and then would throw themselves on the mercy and grace of God through the sacrifices. However, the majority in Israel did the very opposite. They actually made a law out of trying to keep the law and, thereby, instituted a religion of ethics, which, in reality, was no salvation at all.

BUT WHERE SIN ABOUNDED, GRACE DID MUCH MORE ABOUND

The heading sums up the entirety of this scenario as delineated by Paul. Even though sin was rampant from the very beginning (after the fall) and then abounded to mountainous proportions after the law was given, still, grace abounded even more, much more.

Paul actually said, "Where sin increased, grace superabounded, and then some on top of that." However, just because grace abounded, it did not and does not mean that one is free to sin. Paul addresses this in the next chapter.

The idea is that irrespective of how bad sin is in the life of an unbeliever, and irrespective of its depths, its depravity, its death, or its horror, there is always enough of the grace of God to cleanse the sinner of all sin. This, in effect, sets the captive free, that is, if the sinner will throw himself on the mercy and grace of God. Regarding the believer, grace never gives a license to sin, but rather liberty to live a holy life, for grace has power.

As it regards the law of Moses, nothing about that law is incumbent upon believers. Jesus settled it all at Calvary's Cross. It is the Holy Spirit now who leads us and guides us, which He always does according to the Word of God. Yes, if something was morally wrong 3,000 years ago, it is still morally wrong, and to be sure, the Holy Spirit will point it out. As well, we will find it in the Word. Yes, there are things we do and don't do, which should be obvious, but we are not beholden to the law of Moses, and we should understand that.

As well, we should understand that the Holy Spirit is a far stricter guide than the law of Moses. To use as an illustration, a traffic cop on a motorcycle standing by the side of the road carries a whole lot more weight than a mere sign delineating a certain speed limit.

The law says that we are not to commit adultery, but the Holy Spirit says that if one even looks at a woman with lust in his heart, in the eyes of God, he has already committed adultery.

THAT AS SIN HAS REIGNED UNTO DEATH

"That as sin has reigned unto death, even so might grace reign through righteousness unto eternal life by Jesus Christ our Lord" (Rom. 5:21).

The heading actually means that sin reigns as king.

Here, sin is personified and refers to a nature—the totally depraved nature of the unsaved person—that reigns as an absolute monarch in his being.

In this passage, *"unto death"* actually means "in the sphere of death." It is not a very pretty picture!

In fact, every action and every thought by the unredeemed are constituted by God as sin. Even those things that seem to be good cannot be but from a wrong motive as it regards the unbeliever.

In fact, the unbeliever is controlled totally and completely, one might say, 24/7 by the sin nature. When Adam and Eve fell, their very nature became that of sin in every capacity. Unfortunately, the sin nature controls most Christians. It is because they do not understand the Cross of Christ as it regards our everyday living for God. Consequently, they do not know how the Holy Spirit works.

In fact, He works entirely from the capacity of the Cross of Christ. It is the Cross that gives Him the legal means to do all that He does within our hearts and lives.

The fact is that we simply cannot live this life as we ought to live it if we try to do it our way. We must do it God's way. What is God's way of life and living?

Please note the following. Even though we've already given this, because of its great significance, please bear with our repetition:

- Jesus Christ is the source of all things we receive from God (Jn. 1:1-3, 14, 29; 14:6, 20).

- The Cross of Christ is the means, and the only means, by which all of these wonderful things are given to us (Rom. 6:1-14; Col. 2:10-15).
- With Jesus being the source and the Cross being the means, then the Cross of Christ (what Jesus there did) must ever be the object of our faith (I Cor. 1:17-18, 23; 2:2; Gal. 6:14).
- With Jesus as the source and the Cross as the means, and the Cross of Christ ever the object of our faith, then the Holy Spirit, who is God and who can do anything, will work mightily on our behalf. He works entirely from the capacity of the finished work of Christ, i.e., the Cross (Rom. 8:1-11; Eph. 2:13-18).

EVEN SO MIGHT GRACE REIGN THROUGH RIGHTEOUSNESS UNTO ETERNAL LIFE BY JESUS CHRIST OUR LORD

The heading presents what Jesus has done in order to save men from this death of sin. It is the Cross.

Sin reigns unto death, and grace reigns unto life, but it reigns through righteousness, i.e., because of God's righteous judgment of sin at Calvary, executed in the person of His Son, the Lord Jesus Christ.

Let us say it again: It is Christ and His Cross that has made everything—and makes everything—possible.

To God be the glory, great things He has done,
So loved He the world that He gave us His Son,
Who yielded His life an atonement for sin,
And opened the life gate that all may go in.

Oh, perfect redemption, the purchase of blood,
To every believer the promise of God;
The vilest offender who truly believes,
That moment from Jesus a pardon receives.

Great things He has taught us; great things He has done,
And great our rejoicing through Jesus the Son;
But purer, and higher, and greater will be
Our wonder, our transport when Jesus we see.

Praise the Lord, praise the Lord, let the earth hear His voice;
Praise the Lord, praise the Lord, let the people rejoice;
Oh, come to the Father, through Jesus the Son,
And give Him the glory; great things He has done.

CHAPTER 6

GRACE

GRACE

"WHAT SHALL WE SAY THEN? Shall we continue in sin, that grace may abound?" (Rom. 6:1)

WHAT SHALL WE SAY THEN?

The question, *"What shall we say then?"* is meant to direct attention to verse 20 of the previous chapter.

To be sure, Paul is not asking these questions because he doesn't know the answers, but rather because of the erroneous interpretations by others that are placed upon the great doctrine of grace as preached by Paul.

The doctrine of grace, especially that which declares justification to be by faith apart from works, excites the enmity of the natural heart. This enmity expresses itself today (as it has from the first) by the outcry of verse 1.

Here, human reasoning conflicts with divine teaching. The latter declares that man is absolutely ruined by sin and wholly unable to restore himself to God's favor by his own machinations. The former teaches that man is not wholly ruined, but that he can, by self-culture, merit God's favor and secure his own happiness. Actually, such is modern psychology.

MORAL EVOLUTION

Moral evolution contains the idea that man can improve himself, with directions given in any and varied ways. Let the reader understand that there is no such thing as moral evolution. In other words, man cannot better himself, irrespective of what tack he might take. Yet, whereas America's pastime was once baseball, it is now self-improvement. It is certainly true that man needs to be improved, and it is definitely true that Jesus Christ, and Jesus Christ alone, can improve an individual, which He does by the born-again experience. Still, man is totally and completely unable to benefit himself in any way by self-improvement. It cannot be done. Yet, while the Lord Jesus Christ down through the centuries has improved untold millions, still, unredeemed man will not believe such, and he keeps trying to do that which cannot be done.

Let us say it again: There is no such thing as moral evolution, meaning that man can gradually better himself. Education cannot do it; motivation cannot do it; money cannot do it; and talent and ability cannot do it—because man is a fallen creature. That's why man must be born again. Even then, man needs to understand that we can be improved as believers, and we certainly need to be, but only by God's method. That method is the Cross of Christ and our faith in the finished work of Christ. This is why it is absolutely imperative that we understand the teaching on the sin nature if we are to see ourselves improved. This is what we hope to explain fully respecting the verse in question.

SHALL WE CONTINUE IN SIN, THAT GRACE MAY ABOUND?

The question was asked by someone, or else, a statement was made by a legalist who did not understand grace, or he understood it but did not believe in grace.

This person was either claiming that he could sin all he wanted and grace would cover it, or he was claiming that Paul was teaching something that gave people a license to sin. No doubt, these erroneous interpretations, willful or otherwise, were coming from all directions.

To be sure, there were not too many in the church of that day (especially those in Jerusalem) who were very much in sympathy with Paul's message of grace. They wanted to continue in the law of Moses and simply add Jesus to that law. So, as stated, a justification that was altogether by faith and totally apart from works did not sit well. It was from this source that most of the complaints arose.

It is highly unlikely that new converts would have developed this reasoning. The very nature of the complaints rested with those who claimed spiritual maturity.

WHAT IS GRACE?

There are many definitions for grace, but I personally like the following: Grace is simply the goodness of God extended to undeserving people. Grace is made possible by what Jesus did at the Cross. In other words, Christ atoning for all sin made it possible for the Lord to bestow His goodness upon anyone who will simply believe; and that's the key—believing!

The person is to believe that Jesus Christ is the Son of God, and that He died on Calvary's Cross in order for us to be saved and for us to live a holy life.

Many believers understand the Cross as it refers to salvation, as well they should. However, almost none understand the Cross of Christ as it refers to our sanctification—how we live for God on a daily basis, how we grow in the grace and knowledge of the Lord, and how we have victory over the world, the flesh, and the Devil. The truth is, the Cross of Christ has everything to do not only with our salvation but also with our sanctification. We will see it spelled out as we go forward in Chapter 6 of Romans.

SIN

The first thing we must settle regards the word *sin*. Does it refer here to acts of sin committed by the believer or to the depraved nature (sin nature) still in us?

In the Greek text, the definite article appears before the word *sin*, so it actually says, *"the sin."* Therefore, we are referring here to the sin nature, which means that sin is reigning as a king in one's life (Rom. 5:21).

Every time the word *sin* is used in this chapter as a noun, if the reader will substitute the words "sinful nature," "sin nature," or "evil nature" in its place, then interpretation will be much easier.

Someone has said that Romans, Chapter 6, presents the machinery or mechanics of the Holy Spirit in telling the believer how to have victory over sin. That which Jesus Christ did at Calvary and the resurrection is beautifully outlined respecting the believer's position in Christ. That position is not one of attempting to gain the victory, but rather maintaining what Jesus has already done for us.

THE HOLY SPIRIT

In Romans, Chapter 8, we have the dynamics of the Holy Spirit as the source of power that enables the believer to appropriate to himself the great things that Christ has done. In other words, one might say that Chapter 6 of Romans tells us how the Holy Spirit does what He does, while Chapter 8 tells us what He does after we understand how He does it.

In Romans, Chapter 7, we find the self-dependence problem rearing its ugly head, which prevents the Holy Spirit from giving the believer victory over the sin nature. This is what stops the fruit of the Spirit from being developed.

Wuest says, "In this sixth chapter we are presently studying, Paul is not talking about what kind of life the believer should live, but by what method or how he should live that life."

As stated, Romans, Chapter 6, tells us how the Holy Spirit works, while Romans, Chapter 8, tells us what the Holy Spirit does after we understand how He does it.

As Romans, Chapter 8, graphically portrays, we must understand the absolute necessity of the Holy Spirit in all of this. Hopefully, we will learn more about this when we arrive at commentary on that most important work of Paul's.

Actually, it is not possible for anyone to properly understand the Word of God without the aid, leading, and guidance of the Spirit of God. However, when it involves great and salient truths such as we are studying here, and especially considering their complication, it is absolutely imperative that the Holy Spirit have complete control of our lives. He must have this control without interference or hindrance in order that He may perform His office work as He desires. Unfortunately, that is not quite as simple as it sounds.

SHALL WE CONTINUE IN SIN, THAT GRACE MAY ABOUND?

The last question in verse 1 could be asked in this fashion: Shall we continue in the sinful nature? The word *continue* in the Greek is *meno* and means "to remain, abide."

Considering the word *continue,* this question could be asked, as well: Shall we, as believers, continue habitually to sustain the same relationship to the sin nature that we sustained before we were saved? Of course, the answer is no! Yet, many believers are continuing to be ruled by this evil impulse. In fact, virtually the entirety of the church world is controlled by the sin nature. How do I know that? How can I say such a thing?

I say it because the only way to have victory over the sin nature is by and through our faith in Christ and what He did for us at the Cross. I'm not speaking of salvation, but I am speaking of our everyday living for God and the part the Cross plays in this event. The truth is that the modern church knows next to nothing about the Cross of Christ as it refers to our daily living for God. As a result, the modern church as a whole is ruled and controlled by the sin nature, which means their spiritual victory is less, much less, than what it ought to be. Yes, a person can be saved and be ruled by the sin nature. He can be baptized with the Holy Spirit and be ruled by the sin nature. In fact, he can be greatly used of God and still be ruled by the sin nature. Even though that is correct, still, that's not God's way. His way is that the sin nature not have dominion over us in any capacity (Rom. 6:14).

When Paul asked the question, *"Shall we continue in sin, that grace may abound?"* he was not speaking so much with regard to particular acts of sin, but with respect to the believer's relationship to the sin nature. After all, the basic acts of sin in one's life result from the degree that one yields to the sin nature.

WHAT IS THE SIN NATURE?

When Adam and Eve fell in the garden of Eden, their very nature became that of sin. In other words, from then on, everything they did was labeled by God as sin, and I mean everything. They fell from the lofty position of total God-consciousness down to the far, far lower level of total self-consciousness. In other words, everything about their beings, as stated, became that of sin. As we have stated, their nature became that of sin instead of righteousness. Due to the fact that Adam was the federal head of the human race, so to speak, this meant that every baby that would be born thereafter would be born with original sin. Every child would have a human nature (as would be obvious) and would also have a sin nature. They would be ruled by that sin nature unless they came to Christ. In fact, all the trouble in the world—the wars, man's inhumanity to man, the direction of much of humanity, the lying, the cheating, etc.—is all caused by the sin nature ruling individuals. The tragedy is that the sin nature can continue to rule the believer, as we've already stated, and will rule the believer if he doesn't understand God's prescribed order of victory.

One might say that the sin or evil nature is actually the Adamic nature, which imprisoned man at the fall. It has poisoned the entirety of the human race for all time. It is the nature that encourages sin, against which man is powerless.

At Calvary Jesus broke the hold of this deadly yoke; however, He did allow it to remain, though powerless, as a disciplinary measure. If the believer correctly follows Christ, there is no problem; however, if we yield to temptation and to sin and then try to overcome in the flesh, then the sin nature comes alive with serious consequences.

So, in this book we will study this all-important subject of sin in the life of the Christian, why it is there, and the victory afforded by Christ—the only victory there is, incidentally.

DEALING WITH THE SIN NATURE

The following ways are those by which the church addresses the sin nature, if at all. As we will see, only one of these ways is scriptural, and that way is faith in Christ and the Cross—exclusively in Christ and the Cross. The reader must understand that the only answer for sin, and I mean the only answer, is the Cross of Christ. Unfortunately, man has been ever attempting to create another god other than the Lord of Glory, while the church has ever been attempting to perfect another sacrifice other than the Cross.

IGNORANCE

Please note the following very carefully: The truth is that virtually the entirety of the church world (and I speak of those who truly know the Lord) knows nothing at all about the sin nature. Many have never heard a sermon in all of their lives regarding this problem, and this means that most know absolutely nothing about it. As stated, they are ignorant of the sin nature, despite the fact that this is one of the most important factors in the heart and life of the believer. They are ignorant simply because this subject is not preached behind the pulpit because most preachers don't know anything about it either. Faith comes by hearing and hearing by the Word of God. So, if something is not preached, then there is no way that the people can understand as they should. Consequently, I pray that what we teach you in this volume will open your eyes to this very serious problem and help you to obtain victory, especially considering that the Lord has already won for us this great victory, which He did at Calvary.

DENIAL

There are some few who have heard of the sin nature, and we speak of preachers, but they claim that it does not exist in the believer. They claim that it may have existed once before conversion, but when the person is saved, they say that the believer no longer has a sin nature.

The truth is that every believer in the world has three natures:

1. The human nature
2. The sin nature
3. The divine nature

Now, my answer to their claim is this: if the believer doesn't have a sin nature, then why did the Holy Spirit through the apostle Paul take up so much time explaining this thing if it doesn't exist?

Others would ask the question as to why the Lord doesn't remove the sin nature at conversion. As we have previously stated, the Lord leaves the sin nature, although dormant, in the heart and life of the believer for disciplinary purposes. In other words, it's like an electrical appliance that's not plugged in. As long as it remains that way, it causes no problem.

Please notice the following very carefully: When the believer comes to Christ, the sin nature is made completely and totally dormant. In other words, it is not active at all.

So, how does it become active again in the heart and life of the believer?

When a person comes to Christ, he personally thinks that he will never sin again. In fact, sin is a horrible thing to him at this time, and should be. However, he then finds to his chagrin that he does fail the Lord in some way, and it scares him. He is then determined not to do the same thing again, and this is where the problem comes in.

Instead of placing his faith in Christ and the Cross, he places it in something else, and that's when the sin nature is activated. It becomes very confusing to the believer because he desires to live a pure and holy life (even as Paul did in Romans, Chapter 7); however, he finds now that he cannot do what he wants to do, which is to live as he should live. In other words, the sin nature is now controlling such a believer, and if the problem is not rectified with the right teaching, it will get worse and worse.

It's not so much that sin activates the sin nature—it doesn't—rather it's the wrong placement of our faith. We must ever understand that the Cross of Christ, as stated, is the answer to all sin, whether in the believing sinner coming to Christ or the believing Christian trying to live for God. The Cross of Christ is the answer, and the only answer. Until the believer places his or her faith exclusively in Christ and the Cross, and maintains it exclusively in Christ and the Cross, regrettably, the sin nature will rule in the heart and life of such a believer. Yes, the believer is still saved and even Spirit-filled, but he is living far beneath his spiritual privilege in Christ.

LICENSE

As stated, there are some few who do know a little something about the sin nature, but they somehow use it as an excuse to sin. In other words, they think that they have a sin nature; therefore, they can't help but sin. So, they're constantly saying (at least every night), "Lord, forgive me my many sins today." They don't try to overcome sin but take it for granted that they have to sin a little bit each and every day. Nothing could be more wrong. The Lord does not save us *in* sin, but rather He saves us *from* sin. This we must ever understand.

Paul answered this very readily when he said, *"What shall we say then? Shall we continue in sin, that grace may abound?"* His answer was to the point: *"God forbid. How shall we, who are dead to sin, live any longer therein?"* (Rom. 6:1-2).

STRUGGLE

Then there is the group who has a little understanding of the sin nature, and yet again, they may not have any understanding of it at all. They think that the Christian experience is to be a struggle, and in their hearts, they think that somehow this struggle equates to holiness. Never mind that they are failing and will continue to fail. They judge everything by their struggle.

That's not Christianity. If we are struggling with sin, after awhile, we are going to fail. Our struggle is rather to be with faith. We fight the good fight of faith, and that is where the struggle comes in. It is always with our faith. Let me say it again: If we are struggling with sin, we are fighting the wrong fight. We are fighting a fight that's already been fought and won, which was done by Jesus Christ at Cavalry nearly 2,000 years ago.

That's where the struggle comes in. If Satan can get us to lose our faith or to throw over our faith, then he has won the battle. That's where the conflict is. That's where the struggle is. It should not be a struggle with sin. If it is, as we have stated, we have already lost that struggle. In other words, we are trying to wrestle with something that Jesus has already defeated. It must insult the Lord greatly for us to try to do what we cannot do, which, in reality, He has already done.

As we've already stated, there is a struggle, but it should be a struggle with our faith. If we properly understand that, then we can win this conflict.

I suppose that all of us, and I speak of those who truly love the Lord, have faced this battle in our lives. The harder we have to fight, the harder we have to struggle with sin. We think that denotes some type of holiness or consecration. In fact, we take great pride in our struggle—how we are struggling, where we are struggling, and with what we are struggling—and we find to our dismay that it only leads to self-righteousness. All of us have tried to fight battles that Jesus has already fought and won at the Cross. As we've stated, this must be a tremendous insult to the Lord. We are trying to do what we cannot do, and which He has already done.

The problem with all of this is that we are trying to do ourselves simply what cannot be done. It's hard for us to admit that. We think, If I try just a little harder. In fact, that is one of the favorite watch words of preachers when approached by someone struggling: "You've got to try harder." No, trying harder is not the answer. Proper faith is the answer. When we say proper faith, we are talking about the proper *object of* faith, which must be the Cross of Christ.

GRACE

Of all the things we have named, grace is the only means by which we can walk in victory.

Let me explain: The Lord wants to give us good things. He desires to do so. He loves us very, very much. He doesn't require very much of us, but He does require one thing, and that is that our faith be exclusively in Christ and the Cross. If that's not the case, then it's sin.

Paul said, *"For whatsoever is not of faith is sin"* (Rom. 14:23).

By evidencing faith in Christ and the Cross—and maintaining faith in Christ and the Cross—the Holy Spirit, who is God and who can do all things, will then work grandly on our behalf.

Unfortunately, most believers take the Holy Spirit for granted. He will do what He wants to do, and that's it, or so they think.

In fact, the Holy Spirit is dependent upon our faith and the correct object of our faith, which must be the Cross of Christ. It is the Cross of Christ that gives the Holy Spirit the legal means to do all that He does within us and for us.

Paul also said, *"For the law of the Spirit of life* (the Holy Spirit) *in Christ Jesus* (what He did for us at the Cross) *has made me free from the law of sin and death"* (Rom. 8:2). This spells it out for us in no uncertain terms.

The Holy Spirit (please read this carefully) works exclusively within the parameters of the finished work of Christ, and He will work no other way. For us to have His power on our behalf, our faith must ever be placed and maintained in Christ and the Cross. As we've already stated, there is no other place for sin but the Cross.

As a believer, we are facing the powers of darkness, which are much stronger than we are. In fact, there's only one way they can be overcome, and that is by our faith in Christ and His work at Calvary's Cross. If we try to overcome sin or the powers of darkness any other way, no matter how hard we try, ultimately, we will fail.

So, once our faith is rightfully placed and rightfully maintained, then God will grant us His grace and do so in an unlimited supply. In other words, whatever it is that we need, He will do it.

Now let me say it again: the Lord does not demand a lot from us, but He does demand one thing, and that is that our faith ever be in Christ and the Cross, which means that it is to be maintained in Christ and the Cross (I Cor. 1:17-18, 23; 2:2; Rom. 8:1-11; Gal. 6:14; Col. 2:10-15).

UNDERSTANDING ROMANS, CHAPTER SIX

The key to understanding this great chapter is the definite article—a rule of the Greek language in which the New

Testament was originally written—that precedes the word *sin* of verse 1 in the Greek text. In effect, it says *"the* sin."

A rule of Greek syntax refers the sin mentioned in this verse back to the sin mentioned in Romans 5:21. In that verse, sin is looked upon as reigning as a king, and it is clear that the reference there is to the sinful nature, not to acts of sin as we have already explained.

Now, we might be quick to ask why the King James translators did not use the definite article as it is in the original text.

In English, it is somewhat clumsy. Let me explain: Using Romans 6:1 as an example, Paul said, *"What shall we say then? Shall we continue in the sin, that grace may abound?"* That's the way it is in the original text. However, when it is translated into English, it is clumsy to use the word *the* in front of the word *sin* as it was originally given. So, the King James translators left it off. However, whenever Paul uses sin as a noun, as previously stated, he isn't talking about acts of sin, but rather the sin nature. In fact, in Chapter 6 of Romans alone, he mentions sin some 17 times. Fifteen of those times the definite article is placed in front of the word *sin*, making it read *"the* sin,*"* which is referring to the sin nature.

The sin or evil nature is actually the Adamic nature that imprisoned man at the fall. It has poisoned the entirety of the human race for all time. It is the nature that encourages sin, and against which man is powerless. While in verse 14, it does not contain the definite article, still, the word *sin*, as used in that verse, is a noun. So, he is speaking of the sin nature. It is only in verse 15 that Paul speaks of acts of sin.

GOD FORBID

"God forbid. How shall we, who are dead to sin, live any longer therein?" (Rom. 6:2).

The two words, *"God forbid,"* present Paul's answer to the question: "Away with the thought, let not such a thing occur." His first reaction is an emotional one, with his second answer being a rational one.

His answer to the question, *"Shall we continue in sin, that grace may abound?"* is blunt and to the point, and as already stated, *"God forbid."*

Sin is a terrible business, just like cancer. The longer it remains, the more it grows.

HOW SHALL WE, WHO ARE DEAD TO SIN, LIVE ANY LONGER THEREIN?

The question, *"How shall we, who are dead to sin, live any longer therein?"* portrays in a nutshell the hardcore principle of what the believer now is in Christ. Please allow me to emphasize again that Paul is speaking of a spiritual quality that the believer has at the moment of salvation, which is that he is now dead to sin. However, the Christian must remember that death is not extinction but separation.

When Paul asked how it is possible for the believer to continue in sin, he was not asking a question for information, but was rather presenting a rhetorical question designed to declare the impossibility of the thing. He was actually saying that it is an

impossibility for a Christian to habitually sustain the same relationship to the evil nature that he sustained before God saved him.

If a person subscribes to the sin-a-little-bit-every-day religion,
claiming that the believer sins just as much as the unbeliever,
that is a sure sign that this person has never really been born
again. Actually, the new nature (divine nature) is the prime
characteristic of the child of God; however, at the same time,
the evil nature (sin nature) also remains in the believer, which
is the cause of Paul's treatment of this subject.

THE CHRISTIAN AND SIN

The Christian has died to sin in the sense that God (in supernatural grace), while leaving the sinful nature in the believer,
has separated him from it. There has been a definite cleavage (a
disengagement) of the person from the effects of the evil nature,
even though it is still present in the believer. However, this evil
nature, or sin nature, is a dethroned monarch so to speak. Before
salvation, it was the master of the individual. Since salvation,
the believer is its master, that is, if we function God's way. If
not, the sin nature will rule us just as it did before salvation.
No, that doesn't mean that such a believer is not saved, but it
does mean that such a believer is living far beneath that which
the Lord intends.

When the believer begins to see this truth, he has isolated
this nature, identified it and its proper character, and has within
his grasp the remedy for it. The remedy is the Cross of Christ,
and the remedy is only the Cross of Christ. There is no other.

As we have previously stated, most believers (virtually all) have absolutely no understanding whatsoever regarding the Cross as it pertains to our everyday living for God. They address the Cross of Christ relative to salvation and leave it there. They do not understand that the Cross plays just as much a part in our everyday living as it did in our initial salvation. As we have previously stated, the Lord does not require much of us, but He does require one thing, and on that He will not bend. He demands that our faith be exclusively in Christ and what Christ did for us at the Cross. It was at the Cross where all demon spirits and fallen angels were defeated, including Satan himself, and it was at the Cross where all sin was atoned (Col. 2:10-15; Jn. 3:16; I Cor. 2:2). However, if believers do not understand the Cross in this capacity, they will find their living for God will be a series of sinning and repenting, sinning and repenting. While forgiveness is always available to the child of God, and thank the Lord for that, still, that's not God's way. His way is victory.

No, the Bible does not teach sinless perfection. If we understand anything about sin, we understand that. It does, however, teach that sin is not to have dominion over us (Rom. 6:14).

WHY DOES THE LORD LEAVE THE SINFUL NATURE IN THE BELIEVER AFTER CONVERSION?

As previously stated, it is for our discipline.

However, before I go into that a little more fully, let me address myself to some erroneous teaching that seems to be prevalent in some circles.

One particular teaching is sinless perfection. This stems from an erroneous understanding of sanctification. Such teaching claims that a person comes to Jesus at conversion, and then sometime later, hopefully soon, the individual is then sanctified. At that time, at least according to this teaching, the person reaches sinless perfection. Actually, this doctrine came out of the old holiness teaching and is carried over into some Pentecostal circles.

As we've already stated, the Bible does not teach sinless perfection, and as we've also stated, it does teach that sin is not to have dominion over us (Rom. 6:14). The dominion of sin in the life of a believer is a frightful thing. It is not what Christianity is supposed to be. Sin ruling in a believer's life is because he does not understand the Cross relative to sanctification. Let me say it and continue to say it: The believer can walk in victory with no sin dominating him, but he can only do so by the means of the Cross of Christ. The believer must understand that everything we receive from God, and I mean everything, is made possible by the Cross, and is made possible only by the Cross.

SANCTIFICATION

At the moment the believing sinner comes to Christ, he is washed, sanctified, and justified (I Cor. 6:11).

As we have previously explained, sanctification is a work of grace that takes place immediately at salvation. Actually, it is impossible for one to be justified unless he is first made perfectly clean, which sanctification does. It is a free gift from the Lord.

However, even though the believing sinner is made perfect in Christ because of his faith in Christ, still, the sin nature remains, with the sanctifying process continuing. I am speaking now of progressive sanctification.

Once again, as we have previously explained, the moment the believing sinner comes to Christ, he receives a "standing" in the Lord, which never changes—it is in Christ, so it cannot change. However, his "state" is something else altogether; it changes almost by the hour. This is what scholars refer to (and rightly so) as progressive sanctification. In other words, the Holy Spirit is working in the believer's life to bring his state up to his standing. Actually, it is a lifelong process and will not conclude until the believer is presented *"faultless before the presence of His glory with exceeding joy"* (Jude 24).

One could say and be scripturally correct that one is saved and is being saved, or one is sanctified and is being sanctified.

ERROR

There is another teaching that is quite popular, which claims that the soul and the spirit are saved while the body isn't. Consequently, they claim that when the believer sins, only the body sins and not the soul and spirit. Others claim that it is the spirit only that does not sin, but the body and the soul do sin.

There is no truth to either of these claims. Whenever the believer sins, he sins spirit, soul, and body. That's the reason that Paul said, *"And the very God of peace sanctify you wholly* (progressive sanctification)*; and I pray God your whole spirit* *and soul and body be preserved blameless unto the coming of our Lord Jesus Christ"* (I Thess. 5:23).

Then Paul said, *"Having therefore these promises, dearly beloved, let us cleanse ourselves from all filthiness of the flesh and spirit, perfecting holiness in the fear of God"* (II Cor. 7:1).

If the spirit was blameless, as some teach, then Paul's statement makes little sense.

There is another teaching that claims that sin is a consequence of the law, which disappeared with the new covenant. These individuals seem not to understand that sin existed before the law of Moses, which Paul graphically describes in Romans, Chapter 5.

In this thinking, they teach that any confession of sin by the believer before God is error. Behavior is made right by confessing who one is in Christ Jesus, they say. Forgiveness of sin (I Jn. 1:9) then plays but little part in their present-day experience, at least in their thinking. Their whole concept is that everything is made right by a proper confession, which does not include the confessing of any type of sin or failure. Of course, they deny the existence of a sin nature.

This doctrine is dangerous simply because unconfessed sin is sin unforgiven. No, when John wrote, *"If we confess our sins, He is faithful and just to forgive us our sins, and to cleanse us from all unrighteousness"* (I Jn. 1:9), he was writing to believers, as is overly obvious. In fact, it is not possible for an unbeliever to confess all of his sins, considering that everything he does is labeled by God as sin. No, confession is for believers, while believing is for the unredeemed.

Concerning the unredeemed, John said, *"For God so loved the world, that He gave His only begotten Son, that whosoever believes in Him should not perish, but have everlasting life"* (Jn. 3:16).

THE GRACE REVOLUTION

There is another direction that has crept up in the recent past, which is referred to as the "grace revolution," when it is really anything but grace.

Such teaches that the believer is not to even mention sin ever. If we sin, we do not talk about it and do not ask forgiveness for it, but rather confess that we are the righteousness of God.

They claim that I John 1:9 is for unbelievers. In fact, they claim that the entire first chapter of I John is for unbelievers, which is ridiculous. No, John is writing here to believers.

Actually, this grace revolution thing came out of the Word of Faith doctrine and still carries much of its baggage.

Let us say it again: unconfessed sin is unforgiven sin.

They also claim that the Old Testament was law and does not apply to the new covenant. So, they discount David's prayer for forgiveness. Please note: *"Have mercy upon me, O God, according to Your lovingkindness: according unto the multitude of Your tender mercies blot out my transgressions. Wash me thoroughly from my iniquity, and cleanse me from my sin. For I acknowledge my transgressions: and my sin is ever before me. Against You, You only, have I sinned, and done this evil in Your sight: that You might be justified when You speak, and be clear when You judge"* (Ps. 51:1-4).

Then Jesus prayed, *"Our (My) Father who is in heaven, hallowed be Your name. Your kingdom come. Your will be done in earth, as it is in heaven. Give us this day our daily bread. And forgive us our debts* (trespasses), *as we forgive our debtors* (those who trespass against us)*"* (Mat. 6:9-12).

They teach that Jesus prayed that under the old covenant, so it's not applicable for the present.

All of this is a blatant twisting and perversion of Scriptures, which is an abomination in the eyes of God.

No, a believer who has sinned must confess that sin to the Lord and ask for mercy and grace, which will always be given, along with forgiveness.

As well, one does not have to go through a ceremony or a ritual in order for such to be. One has only in his heart to say, "Lord, I have sinned. Please forgive me," or words to that effect. If sincere, the Lord will always forgive.

Unconfessed sin is unforgiven sin. That means sin confessed to God, not to other individuals.

DISCIPLINE!

As we have stated, whenever the believing sinner comes to Christ, the Lord makes of the person a new creation, with old things passing away and all things becoming new. Still, He allows the sin nature to remain, but it's unplugged so to speak. Of course, the sin nature is not a physical thing, but rather a spiritual thing that is controlled by demon spirits, at least if it is active.

Why doesn't the Lord remove it at conversion?

First of all, the believer must understand that it's not the sin nature that causes the believer to sin. Both Adam and Eve sinned, and they had no sin nature whatsoever. When a believer sins, it's not the sin nature that causes the sin, but it is that which comes out of the evil heart of man, even believers.

Jesus said: *"But those things which proceed out of the mouth come forth from the heart; and they defile the man. For out of the heart proceed evil thoughts, murders, adulteries, fornications, thefts, false witness, blasphemies"* (Mat. 15:18-19).

Then after the sin is committed, the believer sets about to stop a repetition of the failure. Virtually all of the time, he places his faith in something other than Christ and the Cross. That's when the sin nature is revived, as stated, and begins to control the believer.

FOR DISCIPLINARY REASONS

The Lord allows the sin nature to remain in the heart and life of the believer with the intention that it will remain inactive. He allows it to remain, as we have previously stated, for disciplinary reasons. We are quickly made to realize that if we fail the Lord in some way, the sin nature can once again become active, which keeps us humble before the Lord. Let me quickly state that it's really not sin that reactivates the sin nature, but rather the placing of our faith in something (anything) other than Christ and the Cross. That is what activates the sin nature and causes it to control the believer, which is not a very pleasant situation

174 | THE SIN NATURE JIMMY SWAGGART

to be in. As we've already stated elsewhere in this volume, virtually the entirety of Christianity, and on a worldwide basis, is
controlled by the sin nature.

How do I know that, and how can I be so certain about
my statement?

The way that I know it is because of the following: The
believer cannot live a life of victory in the Lord, and we speak
of victory over sin, unless one's faith is exclusively in Christ and
the Cross, and maintained exclusively in Christ and the Cross
(I Cor. 1:17-18, 23; 2:2; Col. 2:10-15; Rom. 8:1-11). Sadly and
regrettably, the modern church knows next to nothing about the
Cross of Christ relative to our everyday living for God. Salvation,
yes. Sanctification, no. While the Bible does not teach sinless
perfection, it most definitely does teach that sin is not to have
dominion over us (Rom. 6:14).

WHAT DOES DOMINION OF SIN MEAN?

Paul said, *"For sin shall not have dominion over you: for you
are not under the law, but under grace"* (Rom. 6:14).

Dominion in the Greek is *kuriauo* and means "to lord, to
be lord of, to exercise lordship over." It also means "supreme in
authority; in control."

It plays out by certain sins being repeated over and over
again and gradually getting worse and worse. In other words,
the Christian cannot stop the thing, whatever it is. So, here we
have the believer, who has the Holy Spirit, and who is greater
than the satanic forces of darkness, but yet, the believer is being

controlled by the sin nature. No matter how hard he opposes the situation, he finds himself losing every time.

As we have already stated, there's only one way that such a believer can find victory. Victory is found only in the Cross of Christ. Please forgive our repetition, but we feel that due to the significance of the situation, it is necessary.

Unfortunately, the church lurches from one fad to another without success. It lasts a few months, and then it goes to something else.

THE PURPOSE DRIVEN LIFE BOOK

The book, *The Purpose Driven Life*, is a case in point. It should have been obvious that this book held no answers whatsoever, but rather only harm; however, it seems that most did not see that. They thought they could launch out on the 40 days to do whatever the book said do, and at the end of the 40 days, they would find victory. They found no victory simply because victory cannot be found in that fashion. Once again, victory, as salvation, is found only in the Cross of Christ, and that book definitely does not recommend the Cross.

Until the believer places his or her faith exclusively in Christ and the Cross, and maintains it accordingly, the sin nature will continue to rule such a person. Yes, a person can be saved and be ruled by the sin nature. A person can be baptized with the Holy Spirit and be ruled by the sin nature. Yes, again, a person can be used of the Lord, sometimes greatly, and still be ruled by the sin nature. A person is not saved because he understands the sin nature as he should, but rather he is saved because of his faith in Christ. Millions have their faith in Christ even as they should, but it is only for salvation, and then they try to live for God by the means of the flesh, which cannot be done.

There will come a day when the believer will have no more sin nature. This will occur:

- When the believer dies. Then, of course, there is no more sin nature.
- When the rapture takes place. The Scripture says that every believer alive in the world *"shall be changed. For this corruptible* (sin nature) *must put on incorruption* (a glorified body with no sin nature)*, and this mortal* (subject to death) *must put on immortality* (will never die)*"* (I Cor. 15:52-53).

However, the believer doesn't have to wait for death or the rapture to rid himself of the problem of the sin nature. The Lord has made a way, and that way is the Cross of Christ.

DEAD TO SIN

When we say "dead to sin," we are speaking of being dead to the sin nature. If we are dead to something, there is no activity whatsoever.

Physical death is the separation of a person from his body, while spiritual death is the separation of a person from God.

Being dead to sin doesn't mean that the believer will never sin again, but it does mean that the believer is not dominated by the sin nature. There is a difference in inadvertent sin, whatever it might be, than being controlled by the sin nature, which presents itself as a miserable existence.

Listen again to Paul as he outlines the believer who is controlled by the sin nature:

Let not sin (the sin nature) *therefore reign* (rule) *in your mortal body* (showing that the sin nature can once again rule in the heart and life of the believer, if the believer doesn't constantly look to Christ and the Cross; the 'mortal body' is neutral, which means it can be used for righteousness or unrighteousness), *that you should obey it in the lusts thereof* (ungodly lusts are carried out through the mortal body if faith is not maintained in the Cross [I Cor. 1:17-18]).

Neither yield you your members (of your mortal body) *as instruments of unrighteousness unto sin* (the sin nature): *but yield yourselves unto God* (we are to yield ourselves to Christ and the Cross; that alone guarantees victory over the sin nature), *as those who are alive from the dead* (we have been raised with Christ in 'newness of life'), *and your members* (members of your physical body) *as instruments of righteousness unto God* (this can be done only by virtue of the Cross and our faith in that finished work, and faith which continues in that finished work from day-to-day [Lk. 9:23-24]) (Rom. 6:12-13) (The Expositor's Study Bible).

We as believers are dead to sin only as the Cross of Christ is the object of our faith, and remains the object of our faith.

THE CROSS OF CHRIST

As we have previously stated and will continue to state, the problem is believers not understanding the Cross of Christ as it regards how we live for God on a daily basis. When it comes to salvation, "Jesus died for me" is the greatest statement anyone could ever make, but still, it is the end of the knowledge respecting what Jesus really did. Most Christians have never heard a message—unless they heard it over the SonLife Broadcasting Network—as it regards the Cross respecting their sanctification. Consequently, and as previously stated, the church lurches from one fad to another.

As it regards the Cross, let's read carefully what Jesus said:

And He (Jesus) *said to them all, If any man will come after Me* (the criteria for discipleship), *let him deny himself* (not asceticism as many think, but rather that one denies one's own willpower, self-will, strength, and ability, depending totally on Christ and what He did for us at the Cross), *and take up his cross* (the benefits of the Cross, looking exclusively to what Jesus did there to meet our every need) *daily* (this is so important, our looking to the Cross, that we must renew our faith in what Christ has done for us, even on a daily basis, for Satan will ever try to move us away from the Cross as the object of our faith, which always spells disaster), *and follow Me* (Christ can be followed only by the believer looking to the Cross, understanding what it accomplished, and by that means alone [Gal. 6:14;

Eph. 2:13-18; Col. 2:10-15]) (Lk. 9:23) (The Expositor's
Study Bible).

Jesus then said:

And whosoever does not bear his Cross (this does not speak of
suffering as most think, but rather ever making the Cross of
Christ the object of our faith; we are saved and we are victorious not by suffering, although that sometimes will happen,
or any other similar things, but rather by our faith, but always
with the Cross of Christ as the object of that faith), *and come
after Me* (one can follow Christ only by faith in what He has
done for us at the Cross; He recognizes nothing else), *cannot
be My disciple* (the statement is emphatic; if it's not faith in
the Cross of Christ, then it's faith that God will not recognize,
which means that such people are refused [I Cor. 1:17-18, 21,
23; 2:2; Rom. 6:3-14; 8:1-2, 11, 13; Gal. 6:14; Eph. 2:13-18;
Col. 2:14-15]) (Lk. 14:27) (The Expositor's Study Bible).

WILLPOWER

Most Christians try to live for God by the means of willpower. It cannot be done!

Just a short time ago, I heard a lady preacher over television telling her audience that people should ask the Lord to
strengthen their willpower. To be blunt, that's not God's way.
While the will is most definitely important (Rev. 22:17), that
within itself is not enough.

Most believers have it in their minds that the moment the Lord saves them, He gives them a stronger willpower—strong enough to say no to Satan, etc. No! The will of the believer doesn't change at all. As stated, while the will is very important, it is only the trigger, so to speak, to put the actual force into action.

Listen again to the apostle Paul:

For to will is present with me (Paul is speaking here of his willpower; regrettably, most modern Christians are trying to live for God by means of willpower, thinking falsely that since they have come to Christ, they are now free to say no to sin; that is the wrong way to look at the situation; the believer cannot live for God by the strength of willpower; as stated, while the will is definitely important, it alone is not enough; the believer must exercise faith in Christ and the Cross, and do so constantly; then he will have the ability and strength to say yes to Christ, which automatically says no to the things of the world); *but how to perform that which is good I find not* (outside of the Cross, it is impossible to find a way to do good) (Rom. 7:18) (The Expositor's Study Bible).

Now, it must be understood that the time in Paul's life that he is addressing is after he was saved, baptized with the Holy Spirit, and preaching the gospel. It does not pertain to his life and living before his conversion on the road to Damascus. A mere cursory glance at the text reveals that much. No, Paul was speaking of himself after he was saved. He was trying to live for God and failing miserably.

He went on to say, *"For the good that I would I do not* (if I depend on self and not the Cross): *but the evil which I would not* (don't want to do), *that I do* (which is exactly what every believer will do no matter how hard he tries to do otherwise, if he tries to live his life outside of the Cross [Gal. 2:20-21])" (Rom. 7:19) (The Expositor's Study Bible).

Yet, virtually the entirety of Christendom is trying to overcome Satan and trying to live for God by the means of willpower alone, which, as stated, simply cannot be done. The will of man is not strong enough to overcome the powers of darkness, and neither was it meant to be.

GOD'S WAY

I'm going to be as simple as I know how to be in addressing God's way:

- The Cross of Christ. The Cross is the means by which all things are given to us by the Lord. In other words, it is the Cross that has made everything possible, and we speak of what Jesus there did. The wooden beam had no power whatsoever, but it's what the Lord did that places the Cross as the foundation of all that we receive from God.
- Faith. The Lord operates strictly on the principle of faith. However, it must be faith in Christ and what Christ has done for us at the Cross. Every human being in the

world has faith, but it's not faith that God will recognize. Every Christian likewise has faith, but most of the time it's in the wrong object. The believer's faith must ever be in Christ and what Christ did for us at the Cross (I Cor. 1:17-18; 2:2).

• The Holy Spirit. Once our faith is anchored squarely in Christ and the Cross, and maintained accordingly, the Holy Spirit, who works exclusively within the framework of the finished work of Christ (the Cross), will then work mightily on our behalf. However, the tragedy is that most Christians don't have the slightest idea of how the Holy Spirit works (Rom. 8:1-11). Without fail, the Holy Spirit demands that our faith be in Christ and the Cross.

Paul said:

For the law (that which we are about to give is a law of God, devised by the Godhead in eternity past [I Pet. 1:18-20]; this law, in fact, is 'God's prescribed order of victory') *of the Spirit* (Holy Spirit, i.e., 'the way the Spirit works') *of life* (all life comes from Christ but through the Holy Spirit [Jn. 16:13-14]) *in Christ Jesus* (anytime Paul uses this term or one of its derivatives, he is, without fail, referring to what Christ did at the Cross, which makes this 'life' possible) *has made me free* (given me total victory) *from the law of sin and death* (these are the two most powerful laws in the universe; the 'law of the Spirit of life in Christ Jesus' alone is stronger than the 'law of sin and death'; this means that if the believer attempts to live for God by any manner other than faith in Christ and the Cross, he is doomed to failure) (Rom. 8:2) (The Expositor's Study Bible).

In sin I kept on going
Toward the depths of dark despair,
Each day my sin kept growing,
And my days were filled with care;

But then I heard of Jesus,
And I went to Him in prayer,
And by His grace I found a place among the blest.
I found a place beyond my care.

Alone and brokenhearted,
With no friend to care for me,
For friends had all departed,
Life was hopeless as could be;

Till one day Christ imparted
His own love and made me free,
And by His grace I found a place among the blest,
I found a place for me.

My heart was sorely aching,
And I knew not what to do;
My faith in man was shaking
And the world was looking blue;

I turned, all sin forsaking,
Now I know I'm going through,
For by His grace I found a place among the blest,
And you can find a place just for you.

CHAPTER 7

BAPTISM

BAPTISM

"KNOW YOU NOT, that so many of us as were baptized into Jesus Christ were baptized into his death?" (Rom. 6:3).

DO YOU NOT KNOW THAT SO MANY OF US AS WERE BAPTIZED INTO JESUS CHRIST...

This plainly tells us that this baptism is into Christ and not water (I Cor. 12:13; Gal. 3:26-27; Eph. 4:5; Col. 2:10-15).

The word *baptism* in the Greek here is *baptisma,* which is slightly different than the normal word for baptism, which is *baptizo.*

Here, and in the balance of this chapter, every time this word is used, Paul is using it figuratively. It can be used literally or figuratively. Let me show you how it is used both ways in one verse.

John the Baptist said, *"I indeed baptize you with water unto repentance* (this presents the word *baptized* used literally)*: but He who comes after me is mightier than I, whose shoes I am not* *worthy to bear: He shall baptize you with the Holy Spirit, and with fire* (here John uses the word figuratively)*"* (Mat. 3:11).

The Holy Spirit chose the word *baptize,* or one of its derivatives, because it says what the Divine Spirit wanted said. If one wants to see or know what baptism really means, one only has to look at a ship that has sunk and is lying on the bottom of the river or ocean. The ship is in the water, and the water is in the ship. That is baptism.

When we come to Christ, we are in Christ, and Christ is in us.

Jesus said concerning this: *"At that day* (after the resurrection and the coming of the Holy Spirit on the day of Pentecost) *you shall know that I am in My Father* (speaks of deity—Jesus is God!), *and you in Me* (has to do with our salvation by faith), *and I in you* (enables us to live a victorious life)*"* (Jn. 14:20).

WERE BAPTIZED INTO HIS DEATH?

The entirety of the Bible stretches toward the great book of Romans and, more particularly, Chapter 6 of Romans. When one reads and studies Chapter 6, one is studying the very muscle and sinew of salvation—the new covenant. It tells us how that we are saved, and how we live a victorious life on a daily basis with Christ.

When we came to Christ and, thereby, exhibited faith in Christ and what He did for us at the Cross, in the mind of God, we were literally placed in Christ on the Cross, and we died with Him. Of course, while the death of Christ was physical, our death was spiritual. We died to the old man, we died to the

Adamic nature, we died to sin, we died to Satan, and we died to all that is contrary to the Word of God.

In fact, that's the only thing that God could accept. Had we not died with Him, been buried with Him, and rose with Him from the dead, God could not accept us. He accepts us on the basis of the crucifixion and resurrection of Christ.

Please understand that when we speak of the Cross, we are not speaking of a wooden beam on which Jesus died. We are speaking of what He there accomplished. What did He there do?

First and foremost, Christ atoned for all sin in the giving of Himself as a sacrifice. That means all sin—past, present, and future—at least for all who will believe (Jn. 3:16).

SIN

Sin provides the legal means that Satan has to hold man captive. That's the reason for 20 million alcoholics in America today, and only God knows how many around the world. The same could be said for any other vice or power of darkness. That's the reason it's well-nigh impossible for man to break out of this bondage, this shell, this prison—and a prison it is.

However, with all sin removed, which Jesus did at the Cross, Satan has no more legal right to hold anyone captive. So, if that is the case, and it definitely is, how is it that most of the world is in bondage of some sort? Even believers fall into this category.

The bondage is there, irrespective if the person is an unbeliever or a believer, simply because he does not take advantage of what Jesus did for us at the Cross. The unredeemed out there, for the most part, simply don't believe in Christ and prefer to stay in their captivity, which will ultimately lead to eternal death—the lake of fire.

BELIEVERS

Regrettably, the far greater majority (almost all) of believers are also in a state of bondage in some way. It's the same with the believer as it is the unbeliever. The believer must also take advantage of what Christ has done for us at the Cross by evidencing faith in His finished work. Then, the bondage is broken.

We've already explained it once, but let me say it again: When the believing sinner comes to Christ, he is instantly cleansed of all sin, with every bondage broken. The sin nature is unplugged, so to speak, and that brother or sister enters into a new living and a new life. Such a believer believes he will never sin again, but finds that very shortly, he does fail the Lord again in some way. It scares him, and he determines to take measures so that it won't happen again. That's where the believer begins to go wrong.

Taking his cue from older Christians or whatever, he places his faith in some work of the flesh (such as fasting), which may be legitimate in its own right but is not meant to take away sin. That is the work of the Cross alone. He places his faith in fasting (or whatever it might be) and then finds to his dismay that there is no victory there. It may be victory for a short period of time, but he finds that he fails again very shortly. It scares him, so he doubles down on whatever it is that he is doing, which makes Christianity a drudge.

A DRUDGE

It now becomes a vicious cycle of sinning and repenting, and sinning and repenting. Regrettably, such a person will not know to place his faith in Christ and the Cross unless he hears somebody teach this great subject. *"Faith comes by hearing, and hearing by the Word of God"* (Rom. 10:17).

Sadly, many Christians skip Chapter 6 of Romans simply because they believe that Paul is speaking of water baptism when he uses the word *baptized.* They reckon that they have been baptized in water, and this does not include them, so they pretty much ignore it. In reality, these are some of the most important Scriptures in the entirety of the Word of God. However, because of an assumption, most never hear or heed this great truth—the single most important truth in the world, and it's given to us in this great chapter.

BURIED WITH HIM BY BAPTISM INTO DEATH

"Therefore we are buried with Him by baptism into death: that like as Christ was raised up from the dead by the glory of the Father, even so we also should walk in newness of life" (Rom. 6:4).

Once again we encounter the word *baptism,* and once again we remind the reader that Paul is not speaking here of water baptism, but rather our baptism into Christ, which took place when we were born again, and as it regards His crucifixion.

We must remember that all baptism is always by burial, regardless of what kind of baptism it is, whether water (Acts 8:38), or into Christ. That's the reason that it is necessary for the one being baptized into water to be completely immersed under the water instead of sprinkling.

So, when Jesus died on Calvary and was placed in the tomb—a form of burial—in effect, the believing sinner died with Him and was buried with Him. Actually, that was the entire purpose of Calvary. Jesus would take our place, die, and be buried in our stead, with simple faith in Him awarding the believer what Jesus did. The believer must always understand that the Lord did all of this exclusively for sinners. In other words, nothing in heaven needed such a thing, and above all, God certainly did not need such a thing; however, His love was so great for fallen humanity that He would become man (Isa. 7:14), in effect, be the representative man of the human race. He would then do for us what we could not do for ourselves.

PERFECTION

A thrice-holy God can accept nothing less than perfection. So, with that being the case—and it definitely is—where does it leave man, who is grossly imperfect? It leaves him trusting Christ, who is perfect.

Let's look at it a little closer. Many people do not understand the perfection that God demands and, in effect, *must* demand.

First of all, He demands a perfect birth. In other words, due to Adam's fall, which included every human being who would ever live (with the exception of the Lord Jesus Christ), being born in original sin automatically doomed the human race (which is what Satan knew). However, it seems that Satan never dreamed that God would do what He did, literally become man in order to redeem man.

So, the Lord, through the power of the Holy Spirit, would decree that Mary would become pregnant, which she did. Being a virgin, consequently, having never known man, there was no hint of the fall about Jesus' birth. In fact, Mary only supplied a womb, or house if you will, for some nine months in order for that holy thing to be born. Consequently, Jesus had no traits of Joseph whatsoever (as would be obvious), but neither did He have any traits of Mary.

In other words, this biological miracle did not use the sperm of Joseph (or any other man) or Mary's egg. Mary simply provided a house for this particular period of time. Consequently, you and I receive the benefits of His virgin birth, which means that God does not hold original sin against the believer.

As well, Jesus had to be born of the Virgin Mary in the manner in which He did in order for Him to be the perfect sacrifice at Calvary, for that alone was what God would accept.

For approximately 33 and one-half years, Jesus walked perfectly, never failing even once, in word, thought, or deed; consequently, the believer is awarded His perfect walk, which fulfills the perfection demanded by God.

Then, of course, at Calvary, Jesus was the perfect sin offering, which paid for man's terrible sin debt, and which we are here discussing (Isa. 53:10, 12).

THAT LIKE AS CHRIST WAS RAISED UP FROM THE DEAD BY THE GLORY OF THE FATHER

The resurrection ratified, one might say, what was done at Calvary. In other words, if Jesus had not been raised from the dead, Calvary would have been in vain, as should be obvious. However, it must be understood that the Cross was not dependent on the resurrection, but rather the resurrection was dependent on the Cross. If Jesus had failed to atone for even one sin, even the slightest sin, He could not have been raised from the dead (Rom. 6:23); but due to the fact that He atoned for all sin, as stated, past, present, and future, this guaranteed the resurrection. In other words, the resurrection was not in doubt.

Preachers speak about Jesus fighting demons to be raised from the dead, but that is not found in the Bible, and that is simply because it did not exist. At the Cross our Lord defeated Satan, all fallen angels, and every demon spirit.

HAVING SPOILED PRINCIPALITIES AND POWERS

Paul also said concerning this:

Blotting out the handwriting of ordinances that was against us (pertains to the law of Moses, which was God's standard of righteousness that man could not reach), *which was contrary to us* (law is against us simply because we are unable to keep its precepts, no matter how hard we try), *and took it out of the way* (refers to the penalty of the law being removed), *nailing it to His Cross* (the law with its decrees was abolished in Christ's death, as if crucified with Him); *And having spoiled principalities and powers* (Satan and all of his henchmen were defeated at the Cross by Christ atoning for all sin; sin was the legal right Satan had to hold man in captivity; with all sin atoned, he has no more legal right to hold anyone in bondage), *He* (Christ) *made a show of them openly* (what Jesus did at the Cross was in the face of the whole universe), *triumphing over them in it.* (The triumph is complete, and it was all done for us, meaning we can walk in power and perpetual victory due to the Cross) (Col. 2:14-15) (The Expositor's Study Bible).

DID SATAN UNDERSTAND THE VERACITY OF THE CROSS?

I don't think he did!

If we look at the prophets of old, their prophecies spoke of Jesus dying, but it didn't really say how.

For instance: *"I will put enmity between you and the woman, and between your seed and her seed; it shall bruise your head, and you shall bruise His heel"* (Gen. 3:15). If it is to be noticed, the Cross is not here mentioned.

Then the great prophet Isaiah said, *"He was oppressed, and He was afflicted, yet He opened not His mouth: He is brought as a lamb to the slaughter, and as a sheep before her shearers is dumb, so He opens not His mouth"* (Isa. 53:7). Again, it tells us that Jesus would have to die, but it doesn't tell us how.

And then, there was that early morning hour when Pilate asked the crowd of Jews what he was to do with Jesus. The Scripture says, *"They all say unto him, Let Him be crucified"* (Mat. 27:22).

It was Satan who put this on the mind of these people to demand the crucifixion of Jesus. If Satan had known what the crucifixion meant, what the death of Christ actually would mean, I cannot see him instigating the situation as he did.

No, he thought such a death would cause all the people to turn against Jesus. The law of Moses condemned anyone hanged upon a tree as being cursed by God (Deut. 21:23).

Was Jesus cursed by God?

No! He was made a curse, and that is totally different than being cursed. The judgment that was the curse was because of sin on the part of the individual, and Jesus had no sin. So, He had to be made a curse, which He was, in our place.

"Christ has redeemed us from the curse of the law, being made a curse for us" (Gal. 3:13).

Satan wanted Jesus crucified because he thought this would mean something else to the people, in other words, that He was not who He said He was. Satan knew that Jesus Christ was the Son of God and was the Messiah, but he did not know or understand the Cross of Christ. So, he would demand the very thing that would do him in.

EVEN SO WE ALSO SHOULD WALK
IN NEWNESS OF LIFE

So, the following is true of all believers:

- We were crucified with Christ.
- We were buried with Christ, which means that all of our old sins and lives were buried with Him as well.
- We were raised with Christ in His resurrection to newness of life. In other words, after conversion, we are not what we once were.

WHAT DOES NEWNESS OF LIFE MEAN?

It means exactly what it says: In Christ, we have a new life. People talk about New Year's resolutions, a new beginning, a new start, etc., but it never happens because it cannot happen outside of Christ. However, when the person comes to Christ and is born again, this newness of life comes to the believer. Before conversion, such a person walked in death, but now he walks in life. Sin brings nothing but death—death to our marriages, death to our lives, death to our businesses, death to our efforts—always death, while Christ brings nothing but life.

So, if anyone wants a new start or a new beginning, giving his heart to the Lord Jesus Christ guarantees that newness of life.

It must be understood that it's not so much a new kind of life the believer is to live, but it's a new source of ethical and spiritual energy imparted to him by God, which enables him to live this life. Paul outlines this in Romans, Chapters 12 through 16.

To have this new life, this resurrection life, one must under-stand that it's made possible by the Cross—and the Cross alone. This means that the believer is to place his faith exclusively in Christ and the Cross and maintain it exclusively in Christ and the Cross. He must understand that everything, and I mean everything, that we receive from God is made possible totally and completely by what Jesus did at the Cross.

OUR WALK

Paul uses the word *walk* quite often as it refers to our life and living for the Lord.

The word *walk* in the Greek is *peripatheo* and means "to order one's behavior, to conduct oneself."

The word *should* as in *"even so we also should walk in newness of life,"* throws us off track somewhat. Even though the translation is correct, still, in our thinking respecting English as a language, the word *should* means that it is something that ought to be done but not necessarily that it will be done.

However, in Paul's statement, it means for certain, it shall be done. Consequently, to help us understand it better, it could be translated, "Even so, we also will walk in newness of life," or better yet, "even so, we also walk in newness of life."

In other words, even as the sinner once walked in the old-ness of death, which was brought on by Adam, the believer now walks in newness of life, which was brought on by Jesus Christ.

However, the bitter truth is that most Christians are walk-ing in only a part or a portion of the newness of life. In other words, they are not at all living in that for which Jesus paid such a price.

THE CROSS

Even though the ingredients for victorious living are given to us right here in the Word of God, regrettably, most Christians are not at all living the life they should live. To be frank, to live less than that for which Jesus has paid such a price does not provide the more abundant life for which He died (Jn. 10:10).

The reason is (as we have already addressed), the believer simply does not know that his victorious living, his walk with God, and his victory over the world, the flesh, and the Devil are all anchored in the Cross. For the most part, the believer doesn't know that. Consequently, as previously stated, the church stumbles from one fad to the other.

Donnie picked up a book the other day and opened it. In big bold type in the middle of the page, it stated (or words to this effect): "If you want to live a life of victory over sin, fast 21 days."

Now, while fasting is certainly scriptural, it is not scriptural in that fashion. In other words, the answer for sin is not fasting. The answer for sin is the Cross of Christ, and only the Cross of Christ.

SO, WHAT SHOULD THE BELIEVER DO?

Please note the following very carefully: First of all, the believer should understand the effectiveness of the Cross of Christ. He has to understand that the Cross is just as necessary for our daily walk with God as it was for our salvation. Regrettably, most believers do not know or understand that. In fact, every single thing we receive from the Lord, and I mean everything until the day we die, was all paid for at the Cross of Christ.

So, the believer must first of all understand the veracity (truth) of the Cross, the power of the Cross, and the victory of the Cross. Understanding the Cross of Christ—this is where the believer must anchor his or her faith. In other words, the Cross of Christ must be the object of one's faith, and it must *remain* the object of one's faith. With that being done, the Holy Spirit will grandly help us. The Spirit of God works exclusively within the parameters, so to speak, of the finished work of Christ, and will not work outside of that finished work. In other words, the Cross of Christ gives the Holy Spirit, who does the doing, the legal means to do all that He does. While the Holy Spirit does not leave us, if we place our faith in that which is wrong, He is greatly curtailed in such circumstances. As stated, He doesn't require much of us, but He does require that the Cross of Christ ever be the object of our faith. With that being done, we will slowly begin to see changes in our lives, changes in our living, changes in the way we do things, and changes that lead to victory (Rom. 8:1-11; I Cor. 1:17-18, 21, 23; 2:2; Gal. 6:14; Eph. 2:13-18; Col. 2:10-15).

CALVARY, THE ANSWER TO EVERYTHING

Most believers have been erroneously taught that their faith in what Jesus did at Calvary was necessary in order to be saved, which is correct, but thereafter, they are told it has no bearing on the believer's life and walk before God. Nothing could be further from the truth.

Also, and to make a bad matter worse, there are some preachers, namely the Word of Faith preachers, who teach that Calvary had nothing to do with one's salvation and has nothing to do with any believer anywhere. They say that the Cross of Christ is no more than "past miseries" and "the worst defeat in human history." They claim that we are people of the resurrection, and as such, Calvary is of no consequence.

Many of them go as far as to eliminate all songs about the Cross, the blood of Jesus, or anything of this nature. In fact, one of their leaders stated emphatically that "the blood (and he was speaking of the blood of Jesus) docs not atone." That's coming perilously close to blasphemy.

ENEMIES OF THE CROSS

Paul addressed this, and I quote from The Expositor's Study Bible:

Brethren, be followers together of me (be fellow-imitators), *and mark them which walk so as you have us for an example* (observe intently). (*For many walk* (speaks of those attempting to live for God outside of the victory and rudiments of the Cross of Christ), *of whom I have told you often, and now tell you even weeping* (this is a most serious matter), *that they are the enemies of the Cross of Christ* (those who do not look exclusively to the Cross of Christ must be labeled 'enemies'): *Whose end is destruction* (if the Cross is ignored, and continues to be ignored, the loss of the soul is the only ultimate conclusion), *whose god is their belly* (refers to those who attempt to pervert the gospel for their own personal gain), *and whose glory is in their shame* (the material things they seek, God labels as 'shame'), *who mind earthly things.)* (This means they have no interest in heavenly things, which signifies they are using the Lord for their own personal gain) (Phil. 3:17-19).

THE SIN NATURE

They also deny the sin nature, claiming that a believer's walk is determined by his confession alone. Consequently, all preaching against sin is banned, with them claiming that any preaching of this nature creates a sin consciousness. In other words, they claim that preaching against sin causes one to become conscious of sin and then creates a desire to sin. So, there is little or no preaching against sin in these particular charismatic circles.

Then others, who really come out of the same genre, claim that believers are to never confess sin to God. They are instead to tell the Lord how righteous they are. They're not to think about sin and are not to confess any sins to the Lord or anyone else, claiming that it was all taken care of at the Cross. It most definitely was taken care of at the Cross; however, for the person who is unsaved to take advantage of what was done at the Cross, that person has to accept Christ. Eternal life has been granted to him or her.

As well, when the believer sins, he must confess that sin to the Lord, and do so promptly. Unconfessed sin is unforgiven sin. One does not have to go through a routine, a ceremony, a ritual, etc. In his or her heart, one only has to simply say, "Lord, I sinned. I did wrong, and will You forgive me?"

He has promised us that He will forgive, and without fail.

"If we confess our sins, He is faithful and just to forgive us our sins, and to cleanse us from all unrighteousness" (I Jn. 1:9).

Then, to try and cover their false doctrine, they claim that Chapter 1 of I John is for unbelievers and not believers. A cursory glimpse at the text completely disproves such foolishness. In fact, the entirety of the Bible, including I John, Chapter 1, was written exclusively to believers.

The Scripture plainly says concerning unbelievers, *"But the natural man receives not the things of the Spirit of God: for they are foolishness unto him: neither can he know them, because they are spiritually discerned"* (I Cor. 2:14).

The truth is (as I trust we have amply proved scripturally), faith in what Jesus did at Calvary is definitely necessary for one to be saved, but, as well, continued faith in that atoning work is also necessary for one's victorious walk before God. In other words, Calvary is not only at the core of our salvation experience but, as well, our daily walk before God. Failure to understand this is simply to fail. Faith in this atoning work regarding our victorious walk is necessary each and every day of our lives and is meant to be that way by the Holy Spirit.

FOR IF WE HAVE BEEN PLANTED TOGETHER
IN THE LIKENESS OF HIS DEATH

"For if we have been planted together in the likeness of His death, we shall be also in the likeness of His resurrection" (Rom. 6:5).

The heading proclaims what happened to the believing sinner when he came to Christ. It tells us that the believing sinner died in Him on the Cross and was buried in Him as well. Actually, this is what takes place in the mind of God. It is a spiritual thing and not physical, as I'm sure such is understood.

This means that the price was totally and completely paid concerning the outstanding debt of sin and sins, with simple faith being all that is required on the part of the sinner in order for this standing in Christ to be freely given.

The old *us* had to die, and the only death that God would recognize was our death with Christ—in Christ when He died on the Cross.

The short phrase, *"Have been planted together,"* in the Greek text speaks of a living, vital union of two individuals growing up together. Actually, the same word could be used of Siamese twins whose bodies are connected at one point, and whose blood stream flows through two physical bodies as it does normally through one. That is the best way to explain this union, and it represents the close union between Christ and the believer. Let us say it again: it is spiritual and not physical.

God actually places the believing sinner into Christ at the Cross to share His death and resurrection. As stated, this is done by faith on the part of the believing sinner. In other words, it happens to every single believing sinner who comes to Christ. We die with Him, we are buried with Him, and we are raised with Him in newness of life.

LIKENESS

The word *likeness* in the Greek text is *homioma* and means "a likeness or resemblance which amounts almost to the same identity, even as close as Siamese twins."

The idea is that the believing sinner and the Lord Jesus were united in a death at Cavalry—His death. It was a vicarious death that had to do with the salvation of the believing sinner from the guilt, penalty, and power of sin. Actually, the sinner's death was one that he, in justice, should have died as a result of that sin, but which, in the grace of God, the guilt and penalty of that sin was borne or carried by God's Son. Both deaths had to do with sin, but from different aspects—Jesus bearing the sin that the sinner has given Him.

WE SHALL BE ALSO IN THE LIKENESS
OF HIS RESURRECTION

The heading means that it is impossible to have one (the benefits of Calvary) without having the benefits of the other (newness of life). In fact, the Cross makes the new life possible.

To believe in Christ implies association with Him in His death and resurrection. In Romans 6:3, His death is called His baptism. He was baptized into death, and all who believe in Him are likewise baptized with Him. This means that we were associated with Him in His death, His burial, and His resurrection, at least that's the way God sees the thing.

Actually, this is what He was talking about in John, Chapter 6, when He said, *"Except you eat the flesh of the Son of Man, and drink His blood, you have no life in you"* (Jn. 6:53).

Jesus was not speaking of literally eating His flesh or drinking His blood, but was using that as a metaphor respecting faith in His atoning work (Jn. 3:16; 6:63).

THE RESURRECTION LIFE

Frances and I began in evangelistic work in the 1950s. Going from church to church, I became acquainted (as would be obvious) with many preachers. Often I would hear them talking about living the resurrection life. Most of the time, they were ignoring the Cross and, thereby, speaking of their preference, which was resurrection. I learned later that almost all of this was coming from the Word of Faith doctrine.

Now, it is perfectly proper for the believer to desire resurrection life and to live that type of life, which is a life of victory, and which God intends; however, there is one thing we must understand: The only way that we can have the likeness of His resurrection—live the resurrection life—is to understand that we have also been planted together in the likeness of His death. In other words, resurrection life is impossible without that understanding. It is the Cross that has made, and does make, all of this possible. There is not going to be any resurrection life if a proper understanding of the Cross of Christ relative to our sanctification—how we live for God on a daily basis—is not a part of our thinking and, in fact, our way of life.

THE CROSS OF CHRIST

Let me say it another way: The Cross of Christ makes everything possible, and I mean everything. This means that every believer is to make the Cross of Christ the object of his or her faith. Let me say it again: What Jesus did at the Cross makes everything possible, and without His sacrificial, vicarious, atoning death, we would now have nothing.

Please note the following: A man once said, "Show me the godliest man or woman in the world today, and if the truth be known, there are enough evil thoughts and evil passions that pass through such a person's heart to condemn that person to hell forever and forever, except for the Cross." In fact, the only thing standing between man and eternal hell is the Cross of Christ.

Please understand that the coming resurrection of all the saints, which will take place sometime in the future and will at that time result in the glorification of our bodies, is not on the apostles' mind. He is not speaking of that coming resurrection. He is writing in a context of sanctification as it speaks of our walk before the Lord now and not in the coming glorification.

To be sure, glorification will come at the resurrection of life, which speaks of every saint of God being glorified; however, Paul's subject does not pertain to that now, but rather the believer's daily walk respecting overcoming victory.

VICTORY

So, I think we should understand from all of this that the Holy Spirit intends for us to live a victorious life and that sin not have dominion over us. While the Bible does not teach sinless perfection, it most definitely does teach that sin is not to have dominion over us (Rom. 6:14). As we've also said, the Lord does not save us *in* sin, but rather *from* sin. There is only one way—yes, I said one way—that the believer can walk in such victory, and that is by one's faith ever being in Christ and the Cross, and maintained in Christ and the Cross.

With that being done, the Holy Spirit will work grandly on our behalf to help us because He works entirely by and through the sacrifice of Christ. In other words, the Cross of Christ is what gives the Holy Spirit the legal means to do all that He does with us, by us, and for us.

To whom shall we go, dear Lord,
To gain eternal life?
We yearn for the soul's reward
From sin and endless strife.

To whom shall we go, dear Lord,
When sorrow comes our way?
No other in pity, Lord,
Will hear us when we pray.

To whom shall we go, dear Lord,
When death is drawing near?
Just trusting in You, dear Lord,
To conquer every fear.

CHAPTER 8

THE OLD MAN

THE OLD MAN

"KNOWING THIS, THAT OUR old man is crucified with Him, that the body of sin might be destroyed, that henceforth we should not serve sin" (Rom. 6:6).

KNOWING THIS, THAT OUR OLD MAN IS CRUCIFIED WITH HIM

The heading refers to the person the unbeliever was before he was saved, which was totally depraved, unregenerate, and lacking the life of God.

Concerning this particular passage, Kenneth Wuest said:

There are two words in the Greek which mean 'man.' The first is *anthropos*, and is a generic, racial term, which is used for a male individual at times, but also has the idea in it of manhood in general and, therefore, includes both men and women. The other word is *aner* and refers only to a male person. The word *anthropos* is the word used by Paul and refers, as stated, to an individual man or woman. As well, there are two words in the Greek which mean 'old.' The first is *archaios* and means 'old in point of time.' The other word is *palaios* and means 'old in point of use.' This is the word that Paul uses. It describes something that is worn out, useless, fit to be put on the scrap pile, to be discarded. Consequently, that describes perfectly the 'old man,' which pertains to what we were before we were saved and, thereby, brought to Christ. Some claim that the 'old man' is Satan. However, as is obvious, there is nothing in the Greek text that even remotely suggests such a thing. The idea altogether speaks of the person before salvation.

THAT THE BODY OF SIN MIGHT BE DESTROYED

This actually refers to the human body. The word *body* in the Greek is *soma* and means literally, "the human body."

The word *sin*, as it is used here, speaks of that monster possessing the human body, at least before salvation. Sin actually begins in the mind but is carried out by the physical body. Considering that the mind has links to the spirit of man, one might say that sin begins in one's spirit.

That's the reason that Paul said, *"Having therefore these promises, dearly beloved, let us cleanse ourselves from all filthiness of the flesh and spirit, perfecting holiness in the fear of God"* (II Cor. 7:1).

(The soul and spirit of man probably refers to the heart as it is used in the Word of God.)

So, the idea that when a person sins, he sins only in his soul and physical body, with the spirit of man being untouched, is erroneous. Whenever a person is saved, he is saved spirit, soul, and body. Whenever a person sins, he sins spirit, soul, and body.

If it is to be noticed, Paul also said, *"And the very God of peace sanctify you wholly; and I pray God your whole spirit and soul and body be preserved blameless unto the coming of our Lord Jesus Christ"* (I Thess. 5:23).

As Paul uses the statement here, the idea is that of sin possessing the human body. As stated, the idea is that Satan uses the human body as the vehicle for temptation and, thereby, the carrying out of sinful desires. The reference is, therefore, to the believer's physical body before salvation, which was possessed, dominated, and controlled by the sinful nature. This most definitely can also happen with believers.

The word *destroyed* in the Greek is *katargeo* and means "to render idle, inactive, inoperative, to cause to cease."

It probably would have been better translated, "That the body of sin might be made ineffective."

Actually, the sin nature is not destroyed in the heart and life of the believing sinner at the time of conversion, but it most definitely is made ineffective.

THAT HENCEFORTH WE SHOULD NOT SERVE SIN

Concerning this passage, Wuest also said, "Knowing this, that our old man, that person we were before we were saved, was crucified with Him, in order that our physical body, which at that time was dominated by the sin nature, might be rendered inoperative in that respect, namely, that of being controlled by the sin nature, in order that no longer are we rendering a slave's habitual obedience to the sin nature."

The idea of this phrase is that the person before salvation literally serves sin. This means that every action by unbelievers is constituted by God as sin, with the person actually being a slave to that monster. Calvary broke the stranglehold of sin in our hearts and lives when we were saved. That stranglehold will remain broken if the believer places his or her faith exclusively in Christ and the Cross, and maintains it exclusively in Christ and the Cross. Otherwise, such a believer will find himself once again being controlled by the sin nature, which makes life miserable, to say the least.

FOR HE WHO IS DEAD

"For he who is dead is freed from sin" (Rom. 6:7).

The heading is not speaking of physical death, but rather the historical fact of a believing sinner being identified with Christ in His death on the Cross.

Wuest also said:

The words 'is dead' in the Greek text have reference to a past action, which, in effect, is a once for all action. Thus we have, 'the one who died off once for all,' that is, off from the evil nature, this being a separation from that nature. It speaks of an action so complete and so final that the Holy Spirit through the apostle used the word 'dead.' If something is dead, that means it has no life in it whatsoever, it's not effective, carries no weight, can do nothing, with no danger from that source.

DEAD TO A CERTAIN THING

The text, as stated, is not meaning that the believer is physically dead, or will be physically dead in the future, but is rather dead to a certain thing, in this case, sin. As we will study in a moment, sin is not dead, as is painfully obvious, but the believer is dead to sin. In his past, which was an unbelieving state, the believer was very much alive unto sin. All of this is now changed. However, due to the way it has been done, which pertains to being dead in Christ, the issue very quickly can become confusing.

IN CHRIST

Paul has laboriously defined this death, its type, and the manner in which it was done. It was all in Christ when He died on Calvary. The believing sinner gains this status not by doing anything, but by simply having faith in something that has already been done, namely Calvary.

Here is the problem area: If, at any point in time, the believer places his or her faith in anything except Christ and the Cross, then he will quickly find himself in serious consequences. This great position—dead to sin—in Christ is so defined by the Holy Spirit that one must remain constantly in Christ, and more particularly, in that finished work, or one will quickly find that he is no longer dead to sin.

A CONTINUED FAITH

All of this means that the faith that got us in must continue to operate on a daily basis in order that we stay in. Once again, I speak of faith in Christ and what He did for us at the Cross. It is always at the Cross (I Cor. 1:17-18), and this is where the confusion comes in. We are not speaking here of salvation, but rather of dominion over sin.

Under conviction by the Holy Spirit, the sinner is quickly made to know how helpless he really is and that he must be totally dependent on Christ for salvation. At that moment, he throws himself on the mercy and grace of God, with his faith in that mercy and grace instantly bringing salvation. In fact, he knows very little about all of the rudiments of which we speak—that exhibiting simple faith guarantees him salvation.

However, once this is done, the believer begins to study the Bible, enjoy the blessings of the Lord, and even goes on to be baptized with the Holy Spirit (Acts 2:4). In respect to this, God begins to bless, as He always does. Now, the danger flags begin to fly.

SPIRITUAL ELITISM

At this stage, and, in fact, all through the Christian experience, it is so easy for one to drift over into a position of spiritual elitism, in other words, dependence on self. Inasmuch as self, at times, is so subtle, especially religious self, the transition is made almost without the believer really realizing that such is being done. Spiritual pride has that propensity. Then the believer finds strange things beginning to happen.

He finds himself being tempted beyond his power to resist. That confuses him, but that's exactly what happens. He then finds himself entering into a realm of sinning and repenting and sinning and repenting.

The problem is—although it's very difficult for him to see this—that his faith has been transferred from the Cross of Christ to something else, and it doesn't really matter what the something else is. That's when the sin nature begins to revive and control the believer. The situation will not change and, in fact, will grow steadily worse until the believer's faith is once again placed in Christ and the Cross, and maintained in Christ and the Cross.

IS FREED FROM SIN

These four words present the believer as being cut loose from the sin nature.

The word *freed* in the Greek is *dikaioo* and means "to justify, to declare righteous, to render or make righteous, acquit of a charge, to absolve." It is a term having to do with the law and the courts of law. Consequently, it deals with the doctrine of justification, which is a legal term. However, in this instance, Paul is not dealing with justification, but rather with the doctrine of sanctification. Therefore, the idea of being set free is used— growing out of the idea that a justified person is set free from the penalty of the law.

Wuest says, "The one, Paul says, who died off once for all from the sin nature, has been set free completely from it, with the present result that he is in a state of permanent freedom from it, permanent in the sense that God has set him free permanently from it, and it is his responsibility to maintain that freedom from it (the sin nature) moment by moment."

GRACE

This which is taught by Paul, and one might quickly add, given to him by the Holy Spirit, is little accepted by the majority of Christianity. In fact, the vast majority of mankind accepts the human doctrine of salvation by merit; a very small minority believes the divine doctrine of salvation by grace. The Lord Jesus Himself said that few tread that narrow way. The reason is that it is abhorrent to human pride.

Let us say it another way: Faith in anything other than the Cross gives credit to man and increases human pride. In other words, works minister to our self-importance. Faith in the Cross alone gives glory to God, which is where the glory belongs, with everything else giving glory to man.

As we have already stated, the believer in Christ, trusting in what He did at Calvary and the resurrection, is now dead to the monster of sin; in other words, dead to the sin nature. He is cut loose or freed from that monster, one might say; however, that does not mean that sin or the sin nature is dead, with both continuing to be very much alive and just as much in existence as ever.

And yet, sin or the sin nature need not be any problem to the believer whatsoever, providing the believer continues to exercise faith moment by moment in Christ and what He has done for us at the Cross.

MAINTAINING THE DISCONNECTION

The Christian is exhorted to maintain that relationship of disconnection that God has brought about between him and the indwelling sin nature. However, God has not taken away the free will of the Christian and, thereby, does not treat him as a machine. It is possible for the Christian to connect himself again to the evil nature by an act of his will or a direction of rebellion or ignorance, thus, bringing the sin nature back into his life.

How is that done?

The sin nature revives whenever the believer places his or her faith in something other than the Cross, and it really doesn't matter what that something is. This stops the help of the Holy Spirit in such a life, which proves disastrous.

SPIRITUAL ADULTERY

Let's say it another way: Paul deals with spiritual adultery in Chapter 7 of Romans. He proclaims a woman who is married to a man, and then she goes and marries another man. It says nothing about divorce, which means that she is now married to two husbands.

He likens it to a Christian who is married to Christ, which we all are, and which means that Christ is to meet our every need. In fact, He is the only one who can meet our every need. However, when we put our faith in something else, in effect, the Lord looks at it as our having two husbands. That constitutes spiritual adultery, and that's the state that virtually the entirety of the modern church is in. Believers are married to Christ (II Cor. 11:1-4) and must look to Him exclusively for all that we need, but all too often, we switch our faith to something else. This is mostly done out of ignorance, but regardless, the end result will ultimately be the same—failure.

ANOTHER JESUS, ANOTHER SPIRIT, AND ANOTHER GOSPEL

As most Christians have never heard of spiritual adultery, likewise, most have never heard of another Jesus. What was Paul talking about?

If Jesus is held up minus the Cross, the Holy Spirit looks at it as another Jesus, producing another spirit, which is made possible by another gospel. In other words, it's something that God will not honor.

Now, please understand: If we seek to separate Christ from the Cross in any way, we're left with *"another Jesus"* (II Cor. 11:1-4).

Our Lord came to this world for one distinct purpose, and that was to go to the Cross. This was the manner in which man would be redeemed. It was a frightful price but, yet, a price that God Himself would pay.

Paul said, *"But we preach Christ crucified"* (I Cor. 1:23).

He did not say, "We preach Christ resurrected, Christ ascended, Christ exalted, etc." which all were true, but rather, *"Christ crucified."*

Oh, yes, he preached these other things, as should be obvious, but the emphasis always was Christ crucified because that's where man's redemption was played out—the Cross of Christ.

Sad to say, but virtually the entirety of the modern church world presently is serving another Jesus. This means another spirit and another gospel.

However, he will not be able to do this habitually, and for various reasons. In the first place, it is not the Christian's nature to sin. He has been made a partaker of the divine nature, which impels him to hate sin and to love holiness. So, we have here a terrible problem—a believer who hates sin, which all true believers do, but at the same time, who is dominated by the sin nature. Such doesn't make for more abundant life.

NOW IF WE BE DEAD WITH CHRIST

"Now if we be dead with Christ, we believe that we shall also live with Him" (Rom. 6:8).

The word *if* would have probably been better translated "since," thus reading, "Now since we be (are) dead with Christ."

In other words, it is a settled, guaranteed position, which will accrue into very positive results.

How are we dead with Christ?

As we have previously stated, when the believing sinner accepts Christ, in the mind of God, that believing sinner is placed into Christ, and in the mind of God dies with Christ, is buried with Christ, and is raised with Christ in newness of life. As also stated, this is not anything physical, but spiritual. Upon simple faith in Christ, the Lord looks at us as dead, meaning that the old man has died. What we once were, we no longer are.

People are fond of speaking of a new beginning or a fresh start; however, it never works simply because what they are beginning with stays with them. It does not change, as it cannot change. However, when a person comes to Christ, what we take with us is crucified with Christ, making it possible for us to truly begin anew. That's the only New Year's resolution, so to speak, that will pass muster.

Every Christian should look at himself as being dead with Christ. As someone has said, "The believer has no past, while the Devil has no future."

WE BELIEVE THAT WE SHALL ALSO LIVE WITH HIM

The heading presents the results of the surgical operation (spiritually speaking) of being freed from sin.

In other words, there was a purpose behind the believer dying with Christ on Calvary and being buried with Him.

Had it stopped there, the work would have only been half done. The purpose is not only to free one from sin with the debt justly paid—even though that is an absolute necessity—but also the end result of the new life in Christ to which the Spirit is pointing.

Consequently, this shoots down the theory that the only difference in the believer and the unbeliever is the blood of Christ. In other words, those who contend for that particular doctrine are actually claiming that believers sin just as much as unbelievers, but the difference is that one trusts Christ while the other doesn't. Nothing could be further from the truth.

While the blood of Jesus definitely is applied to the believing sinner, with all of its wonderful attendant results, still, there is a purpose in all of this, and it is to live the resurrection life free from sin's dominion.

WE BELIEVE

The two words "we believe" proclaim the necessity of the continued use of faith, and more particularly, faith in Christ and the Cross respecting our continued victory over sin. This is absolutely imperative!

We are to simply believe that not only were our sins handled at Calvary, but, as well, the resurrection of Christ guaranteed our victorious walk over and above the dominion of sin. No, this does not mean sinless perfection. That will not come about until the first resurrection of life when corruption will put on incorruption and mortality will put on immortality (I Cor. 15:51-57;

I Thess. 4:13-18). It does mean, though, that the believer is now free from sin's dominion. The believer can stay free and is meant to stay free, but it is done so only by continued faith in Christ and the Cross (I Cor. 1:17-18, 23; 2:2; Rom. 8:1-11; Col. 2:10-15).

THAT WE SHALL ALSO LIVE WITH HIM

The word *Him* is a personal pronoun and means that we live with respect to Him. That is, the believer's new life imparted to him at the moment of believing is life derived from Christ. We live by means of Him. The believer derives his spiritual life from Christ in that sense. Paul is not speaking here of the believer's fellowship with Christ here or in eternity. He is speaking of what Christ did for us and our appropriation of that great victory within our hearts and lives.

How long does the believer derive his spiritual life from the Lord Jesus? It is as long as Christ lives and as long as the believer understands that the Cross is the means by which all of this is done.

Paul says that Jesus died once for all, and that death over Him will never again exercise lordship, thus, the believer is sustained in his spiritual life for time and eternity since Christ is in his life. In other words, as long as Christ lives, the believer lives!

This great divine fact is to be believed and reckoned to be true because it is true, and as a consequence, the members of one's personal physical body are to be yielded to God as weapons of righteousness.

KNOWING THAT CHRIST BEING RAISED
FROM THE DEAD DIES NO MORE

"Knowing that Christ being raised from the dead dies no more; death has no more dominion over Him" (Rom. 6:9).

The heading proclaims the fact that Christ will never have to die again for the sins of man. The reason is that He addressed every sin—past, present, and future—at the Cross. This means that He also won every victory. It also means that He defeated Satan, every fallen angel, and every demon spirit. In other words, there was absolutely nothing undone at Calvary's Cross.

COMPLETE IN HIM

That's the reason that the Holy Spirit through Paul could say the following:

And you are complete in Him (the satisfaction of every spiritual want is found in Christ, made possible by the Cross), *which is the Head of all principality and power* (His headship extends not only over the church, which voluntarily serves Him, but over all forces that are opposed to Him as well [Phil. 2:10-11]): *In whom also you are circumcised with the circumcision made without hands* (that which is brought about by the Cross [Rom. 6:3-5]), *in putting off the body of the sins of the flesh by the circumcision of Christ* (refers to the old carnal nature that is defeated by the believer placing his faith totally in the Cross, which gives the Holy Spirit latitude to work): *buried with Him in baptism* (does not refer to water baptism, but rather to the believer baptized into the death of Christ, which refers to the crucifixion and Christ as our substitute [Rom. 6:3-4]), *wherein also you are risen with Him through the faith of the operation of God, who has raised Him from the dead.* (This does not refer to our physical future resurrection, but to that spiritual resurrection from a sinful state into divine life. We died with Him, we are buried with Him, and we rose with Him [Rom. 6:3-5], and herein lies the secret to all spiritual victory.)

NAILING IT TO HIS CROSS

And you, being dead in your sins and the uncircumcision of your flesh (speaks of spiritual death [i.e., 'separation from God'], which sin does!), *has He quickened together with Him* (refers to being made spiritually alive, which is done through being 'born again'), *having forgiven you all trespasses* (the Cross made it possible for all manner of sins to be forgiven and taken away); *blotting out the handwriting of ordinances that was against us* (pertains to the law of Moses, which was God's standard of righteousness that man could not reach), *which was contrary to us* (law is against us simply because we are unable to keep its precepts, no matter how hard we try), *and took it out of the way* (refers to the penalty of the law being removed), *nailing it to His Cross* (the law with its decrees was abolished in Christ's death, as if crucified with Him); *And having spoiled principalities and powers* (Satan and all of his henchmen were defeated at the Cross by Christ atoning for all sin; sin was the legal right Satan had to hold man captive [ESB says "in captivity]; with all sin atoned, he has no more legal right to hold anyone in bondage), *He* (Christ) *made a show of them openly* (what Jesus did at the Cross was in the face of the whole universe), *triumphing over them in it.* (The triumph is complete, and it was all done for us, meaning we can walk in power and perpetual victory due to the Cross) (Col. 2:10-15) (The Expositor's Study Bible).

DEATH HAS NO MORE DOMINION OVER HIM

The heading presents "dominion" as the key word.

The word *dominion* in the Greek text is *kurieuo* and means "to rule, to be lord of, to exercise lordship over."

The word *death* in the Greek is *thanatos* and means "deadly, or to be dead." In other words, it is a state of being or supremacy.

Death is here spoken of as it relates to sin—*"for the wages of sin is death"* (Rom. 6:23). It speaks of the entirety of the hold over the human race, with all of its by-products of bondage, darkness, absence of life, and in this case, an absence of spiritual life.

The idea is that Jesus' death, which speaks of His poured-out life relative to His poured-out blood, satisfied the claims of heavenly justice. In that the sin debt was satisfied in this act, Satan now has no more hold on the human family, at least those who believe in what Christ did. Therefore, the dominion of death, with all of its attendant results, is broken in the life of the believer who accepts what Christ did.

As death holds no more dominion over Jesus, it holds no more dominion over the believer, and that refers to sin.

As we have repeatedly stated, the idea of all of this that Paul teaches is that sin no longer has dominion over the believer, at least the believer who has his faith anchored in Christ and the Cross. In fact, death and sin are both still a reality and very much in force, and will continue to be until the resolution of all things (I Cor. 15:24-28).

However, the force of both death and sin has no more hold in the believer's life, with its dominion totally and completely broken. This is the miracle and wonder of the new birth, and why Jesus is the only answer for suffering, dying humanity. Every philosophy or religion pales into insignificance, actually, into nothingness in comparison to Jesus Christ and what He did at Calvary.

FOR IN THAT HE DIED,
HE DIED UNTO SIN ONCE

"For in that He died, He died unto sin once: but in that He lives, He lives unto God" (Rom. 6:10).

The heading actually means that He died unto sin once for all.

The sin here, of which Paul speaks, does not refer to particular acts of sin. That aspect of the death of our Lord, namely, that of paying the penalty for our sins, Paul addressed in Romans 3:21-5:11.

Here he speaks of the relation of Christ's death to the sinful nature of the individual. Our Lord's death not only paid the penalty for human sin, but it was used of God to break the power of indwelling sin in the believer's life. That is what the songwriter meant when he wrote concerning the blood of Christ:

Be of sin the double cure,

Saved from wrath and make me pure.

Even though this is very simple, it is something that many believers have never heard, or else, they have not thought of it in this sense.

THE DOUBLE CURE

Considering how important that it really is, please allow us to say it again: When Jesus died on Calvary, the terrible sin debt of man was then paid in full. As we have said it so many times, heavenly justice was then satisfied.

That particular aspect of His death did not really involve the sinner, except in a distant way. In other words, all the sinner has to do is simply believe that, and salvation is afforded.

However, Jesus died not only that the great sin debt be paid, which it was, but also that the believing sinner might be free from the dominion of sin and its effects thereafter. So, as the song says, it was a "double cure."

Now, this last aspect of His death takes on a much more personal nature, even as Paul grandly explains in Chapter 6 of Romans:

- The sin debt was forever paid at Cavalry.
- The dominion of sin is broken in the heart and life of the believer.

It is brought about in relationship to the believer literally dying with Him and, in effect, literally in Him, being buried in Him, and then resurrected in Him. In this manner, the dominion of sin was broken in the life of the believer; however, the sad truth is, the dominion of sin is not broken in the hearts and lives of most believers, despite the fact of what Jesus has done. What is the problem?

THE DOMINION OF SIN

For the believer to have all the benefits of Calvary, which our Lord certainly intends, he must understand the following:

- Every single thing that comes our way from God comes through Jesus Christ, with the means being the Cross. In other words, it is the Cross of Christ that makes everything possible, and especially speaking of the dominion of sin being broken in our lives.

- With that being the case, we must make the Cross of Christ the object of our faith, and the Cross of Christ alone as the object of our faith. It is the same thing as having faith in the Word of God. Actually, the entirety of the story of the Bible, in one way or another, is Jesus Christ and Him crucified. So, as stated, when your faith is in Christ and the Cross, it most definitely is in the Word of God. With one's faith anchored steadily in Christ and the Cross, and maintained in Christ and the Cross, the Holy Spirit, who works entirely within the framework, so to speak, of the finished work of Christ, will then work mightily on our behalf. It is the Cross of Christ that gives the Holy Spirit the legal means to do all of the things that He can do, and He can do anything (Rom. 8:2).

With the believer placing and maintaining his faith exclusively in Christ and the Cross, which guarantees the help of the Holy Spirit on a total basis, then the sin nature, or acts of sin, will no longer have dominion over us. That is God's way, and His only way, because it is the only thing that is needed.

THE MODERN CHURCH

However, the truth is that the modern church puts its faith in anything and everything except the Cross of Christ. Many of the things in which it places its faith are scriptural in their own right, such as fasting, etc., but please understand, sin is the problem, and sin can be overcome only by faith in Christ and the Cross. While fasting is scriptural, it will not give one victory over sin. While memorizing and quoting particular Scriptures is what believers ought to do, still, that will not give a believer victory over sin. In fact, the list goes on and on. It is the Cross alone that provides the victory that all of us want and must have.

BUT IN THAT HE LIVES, HE LIVES UNTO GOD

The first phrase of this verse spoke of Jesus dying once unto sin, and that is all that would be necessary, and now it speaks of Him living, with his life derived from God.

The phrase, *"He lives unto God,"* tells us that all of this was instituted by God, and not by man. As well, it speaks of Jesus doing all of this as the representative man, in effect, for us.

The word *lives* has a triple meaning:

1. It speaks of our daily walk and, consequently, daily victory over sin.
2. It speaks of more abundant life (Jn. 10:10).
3. It speaks of life sustained by God and, consequently, infallible.

Because He lives, we shall live also, and the life and living that is here mentioned is not merely the act of breathing. It actually speaks, just as stated, of more abundant life.

If the believer places his or her faith exclusively in Christ and the Cross, this not only gives eternal life, which refers to abiding with the Lord forever, but also gives a well-rounded life in our living presently. What Jesus did at the Cross paid for it all.

If you from sin
Are longing to be free,
Look to the Lamb of God;
He, to redeem you died on Calvary,
Look to the Lamb of God.

When Satan tempts,
And doubts and fears assail,
Look to the Lamb of God.
You, in His strength
Shall over all prevail,
Look to the Lamb of God.

Are you weary?
Does the way seem long?
Look to the Lamb of God;
His love will cheer
And fill your heart with song,
Look to the Lamb of God.

Fear not when shadows on your pathway fall,
Look to the Lamb of God;
In joy or sorrow Christ is all in all,
Look to the Lamb of God.

CHAPTER 9

DEAD

CHAPTER NINE

DEAD

"LIKEWISE RECKON YOU ALSO yourselves to be dead indeed unto sin, but alive unto God through Jesus Christ our Lord" (Rom. 6:11).

LIKEWISE RECKON YOU ALSO YOURSELVES TO BE DEAD INDEED UNTO SIN

The heading probably comes closer to a formula than anything else found in the Word of God.

If it is to be noticed, the text says that we are *"dead indeed unto sin,"* or rather dead unto the sin nature, but it doesn't say that the sin nature is dead. In fact, it isn't dead. So, how is it that we are dead to the sin nature? We are dead to the sin nature because of what Christ did at Calvary's Cross and that alone. While everything Jesus did was of utmost significance, as should be obvious, still, it was the Cross that paid the price, which gave us the liberty and victory that we now have. So, I am dead to the sin nature simply because of what Jesus did for me at the Cross.

Now, that is what happened at Calvary and my acceptance of Christ; however, the situation is that I remain dead to the sin nature. The truth is that the far greater majority of believers in the world today are not dead to the sin nature, although loving the Lord with all of their hearts. In fact, the sin nature is very much alive and causing them untold difficulties and problems. Why?

It is that way simply because their faith is in something other than Christ and the Cross, and it doesn't matter what it is. If it's not the Cross of Christ, then the sin nature is going to rule such a believer, with the problem getting worse and worse. That is the state of the modern church presently.

Please understand that there is only one answer in the world today for sin, and that is the Cross of Christ. If we choose anything else, no matter what it is or how good it may seem to be on the surface, the sin problem will not be addressed. It is the Cross alone that can and does address the sin problem.

WHAT THE BELIEVER FIRST OF ALL MUST DO

He is to first of all reckon himself to be dead to sin.

The word *reckon* in the Greek is *logizomai* and means "to reckon, count, compute, to take into account."

Why is he dead to the sin nature?

We are dead to the sin nature simply because of what Jesus Christ did at the Cross of Calvary, even as we've already stated. It is not because of how religious we are, what church we attend, how many verses of the Bible we memorize, or how much faith we think we have, etc. It is all because of what Jesus did at the Cross, and that we must never forget. In other words, Calvary paid it all.

The believer must not allow himself to think otherwise. It must ever be the Cross, the Cross, the Cross.

As well we must remember that sin is the problem. Regrettably, we have a habit of following the world with our trying to label sin as something else, such as a mistake, a mendacity, or an error, when all of the time it is sin. We can call it a mistake if we so desire, and then take it some other place, but if we're going to get the help that we must have, we must understand that it's sin—whatever it might be—and that the Cross is the only solution.

BUT ALIVE UNTO GOD THROUGH JESUS CHRIST OUR LORD

Not only is the believer dead to the sin nature through the Cross, and only the Cross, but, as well, he is *"alive unto God through Jesus Christ our Lord,"* which refers to what He did for us at the Cross.

So, what does this mean?

First of all, it means that we never cease to understand that it all comes to us through the Cross, which means that the Cross of Christ must ever be the object of our faith. There our faith must rest, and there our faith must be maintained.

Victory in life and living in every capacity is God's will for His children. It is all made possible by the Cross. If you will notice, we keep saying that because it is true.

Before most believers finally begin to learn the benefits of the Cross, they have to unlearn all types of things in their hearts and lives. In other words, it's an unlearning process, which refers to taking things out that are wrong. Sad to say, most of what believers believe is wrong. In fact, if it is not the Cross of Christ, it is wrong, and it will not bring any blessing or help.

Being alive unto God through Jesus Christ our Lord means that we draw on the life of God, which is unending. This means that we are drawing upon someone who can do anything, who is all-powerful, who is all-knowing, and who is everywhere. Considering the price that Jesus paid at the Cross, don't you think that He wants us to have everything for which He paid such a price? I can assure you that He does.

THE SOURCE

Now, what does *everything* mean?

It means exactly what it says—everything. The Cross of Christ has made it possible for us to have everything.

First, we have eternal life, and there is nothing in the world greater than that. It's the born-again experience. It means that our names are written down in the Lamb's Book of Life.

Second, it means that now the Holy Spirit lives in us, who is God, and who can do anything. He is there to lead us, to guide us, to help us, to empower us, and to help us to realize all for which Jesus died. While He was *with* all believers before the Cross, He is now permanently *in* all believers as a result of the Cross (Jn. 14:16-18).

Now the Cross of Christ makes divine healing possible for every believer.

Last of all, the Cross is the source of any and all blessings. I speak of financial blessings, answers to prayer, and communion with our Lord (above all, communion with our Lord). I might quickly add that there are a thousand other things that I have not mentioned. In other words, as previously stated, we are speaking of more abundant life (Jn. 10:10). The Cross of Christ makes it all possible.

VICTORY AND OVERCOMING POWER

Consequently, the believer is to never talk about trying to get victory over something, trying to be an overcomer, etc. That is wrong terminology and proclaims that the believer does not fully understand what Jesus has done for him at the Cross.

In fact (and it is the truth), even the weakest believer is already victorious in Christ and is already an overcomer as well. However, there are several problems with that. To be sure, the problems are not in the finished work of Christ but in the believer's position in Christ.

First of all, it is very difficult for the sinner to admit that there is nothing he can personally do to effect his salvation but that he must depend totally upon Christ. That is what keeps many, if not most, people from being saved. They keep thinking that they can effect their own salvation in some way.

However, once the sinner comes to Jesus, that problem of self-sufficiency is still in the believer, at least to a certain extent.

All of it is a carryover from the fall in the garden of Eden. As a result, the believer begins to think that he can do something toward effecting his victory in Christ.

SELF-EFFORT

The believer then begins this round of self-efforts, which negates the grace of God and only produces failure, as fail it must. To such a believer, the Christian life is a great struggle, which demands great effort on the part of the believer. He finds himself fighting Satan. That is a battle he cannot win and, in fact, does not need to win considering that Jesus has already won that conflict.

So, it is very difficult for the believer to fully rely on what Jesus has already done at the Cross, or else, he is blind to the fact of what the atonement actually means in Christ. As we have already stated, he knows that Jesus has paid the penalty for sin, but he doesn't quite understand that He has broken sin's dominion. Of course, Satan always takes advantage of ignorance.

Let me say it again: In Jesus, the believer already has the victory and is already an overcomer, that is, if his or her faith is exclusively in Christ and the Cross, and is maintained exclusively in Christ and the Cross. With that being the case, the believer will literally grow into the victory that he actually already has.

If such a believer begins to look to himself, he will find all kinds of things that are wrong. Look to Jesus and the price that

He paid at the Cross, and you will find yourself getting stronger and stronger, with these problems beginning to drop off one by one. However, it is only if our faith is exclusively in Christ and what He has done for us at the Cross.

FIGHT THE GOOD FIGHT OF FAITH

Actually, there is only one fight in which the Christian is to engage, and that is the *"good fight of faith"* (I Tim. 6:12).

The believer is not to fight the Devil, for Jesus has already fought him and won (Col. 2:10-15). Actually, if the Christian is fighting and winning, fighting and winning, after awhile, he is going to fight and lose simply because this is the wrong fight.

The believer is not to fight demon spirits, for they were fought and defeated at Calvary as well. He is to merely resist the Devil and evil spirits by doing the following:

- Placing his faith entirely in Christ and the Cross, and maintaining it entirely in Christ and the Cross (I Cor. 1:17-18, 23; 2:2; Col. 2:10-15). Please understand that when one places one's faith entirely in Christ and the Cross, that is the same as placing it entirely in the Word of God. In fact, the story of the Bible is the story of Jesus Christ and Him crucified.

- Using the name of Jesus. We have the privilege of using the name of Jesus, which is all-powerful (Mk. 16:17; Mat. 28:18).

- Having the Holy Spirit. We have the Holy Spirit in us, who is greater than all the powers of darkness (I Jn. 4:4).

Now, please remember that the Holy Spirit will not function outside of the Cross of Christ. The Cross is what gives Him the legal means to do all that He does for us, but this means that our faith must ever be in Christ and the Cross. Then, the Holy Spirit will grandly work for us.

- Understanding the battle. As stated, every believer must understand that the battle has already been fought and won in every capacity by the Lord Jesus Christ. That's the reason Paul said, *"through Jesus Christ our Lord."*

ONCE FOR ALL

Whenever we try to fight these battles all over again, we are, in essence, saying that what Jesus did was not enough, and our little part has to be added to His effort.

However, Paul also said that Jesus died unto sin once, and, as stated, it means "once for all." His victory was complete and needs nothing added. In fact, whenever we attempt to fight these battles all over again, which we do not need to fight, we stop the grace of God from working on our behalf, which means we are doomed to failure. So, that effort is a losing operation all the way around.

While the believer does fight the good fight of faith, it is from a position of maintaining the victory, and not really trying to gain the victory. As well, we do not try to become an overcomer. In fact, we are already an overcomer in Christ, that is, if our faith is in Christ and the Cross exclusively.

Every believer must understand that if it were possible for us to overcome in our own strength and power, then Jesus wasted His time by coming down here and dying on Calvary. No, there was no way that we in ourselves could effect this great work. It had to be done for us, and it was done by our Saviour.

THE REST THAT THE BELIEVER HAS IN CHRIST

Jesus said, *"Come unto Me, all you who labor and are heavy laden, and I will give you rest"* (Mat. 11:28).

If one is to notice, Jesus did not say that He would give us another conflict or another battle, but rather rest. That means rest from the struggle, rest from self-efforts, and rest from the labor of trying to attain these things in Christ—things that have already been done for us.

When Jesus came the first time, Israel was laboring under the heavy load of the law, which was made even heavier by the added laws (hundreds of them) imposed by the Pharisees. Consequently, living for God had become a terrible chore, which was not the plan of God. Hence, Jesus invited Israel, and the whole world for that matter, and for all time, to come to Him, and He would give us rest.

With many believers, living for Jesus is a battle of immense proportions. In fact, it's a battle they are always losing. The simple reason is that it is a battle that has already been fought and won. We do not need to take the land again; it has already been taken. We do not have to defeat the giants again; they have already been defeated. Actually, that is at least a part of what Calvary is all about.

OPPOSITION TO THE WORK OF GOD

Many believers misunderstand or mistake one's Christian life in respect to one's Christian work. They are two different things altogether.

Respecting our life in Christ, it is to be one that is struggle free. As stated over and over again, the power of the sin nature has been broken once and for all. Sin no longer has dominion over the believer, at least not over the believer who has his or her faith exclusively in Christ and the Cross.

Living for God is supposed to be, and, in fact, is, the most delightful, glorious, wonderful, exciting, thrilling, heavenly, and abundant life that anyone could ever think, contemplate, or comprehend. It is all in Jesus and what He has done for us at the Cross.

However, when it comes to our work for God, that is something else altogether. Satan opposes that work in every conceivable way possible, with Paul as an excellent example.

PAUL

One would have to know and understand that at a point in time, Paul had gained total victory in the realm of living for God. This does not mean that he was sinlessly perfect, for he wasn't, but it does mean that no sin had dominion over him; consequently, I think he would certainly be an example, with Christ as the perfect example. Nevertheless, Satan fought this apostle and, in fact, all of the apostles, concerning their work for God. The truth is, Satan continues to oppose the work of God even unto this very hour.

Paul faced prison, beatings, and stonings, in fact, about every negative thing that one could think, in his efforts to take the gospel of Jesus Christ to a dying world. However, that is altogether different than one's life in Christ. So, the believer must distinguish between the two—one's life and living in Christ and one's work for Christ.

However, having said that, despite the hardships and difficulties that always come to one who is truly working for God, victory in that, as well, is ours as we believe the Lord. Nevertheless, one must not think that this part of our Christian experience—our working for God—is uneventful, for it is not. Some have tried to claim it as such, but they very shortly found out to their dismay that what they were saying was not correct, or else, they really were not working for the Lord to begin with.

The secret is this: Even when Paul was in prison, his personal victory was complete. Even when they were stoning him, his victory and life in Christ were strong and powerful. In fact, these hardships and difficulties could not take away from his personal victory because he knew in whom he had believed and was persuaded that the Lord was able to keep that which he had committed unto Him against that day (II Cor., Chpt. 4; II Tim. 1:12).

THE HOLY SPIRIT

On top of this, and even as we have previously stated, we could not say the following too much or too often: In all of this, our knowledge of what Christ has done for us, our faith in that finished work, and our reckoning it as such must be reinforced and strengthened constantly by the Holy Spirit. In fact, He alone imparts this knowledge correctly to us, and He alone energizes our faith. He is the one who makes our reckoning a reality instead of a mere empty boast. That's the reason that Paul spoke of the Holy Spirit so strongly in Chapter 8 of Romans.

I personally believe that none of these great truths or the victories presented in these truths can be made a reality in the lives of believers without the Holy Spirit. I realize that many would take exception to what I am saying, claiming that the believer is expected to do great things. That is true; however, we can only do such by the help, the leading, the guidance, and the empowerment of the Holy Spirit.

PLEASE NOTE THE FOLLOWING

Just before the ascension of our Lord to heaven, as it regarded His followers, He *"commanded them that they should not depart from Jerusalem, but wait for the promise of the Father"* (Acts 1:4). He was speaking about the baptism with the Holy Spirit.

Then He said, *"But you shall receive power, after that the Holy Spirit is come upon you: and you shall be witnesses unto Me both in Jerusalem, and in all Judaea, and in Samaria, and unto the utter-most part of the earth"* (Acts 1:8).

The power that he was speaking of would only accompany those who would be baptized with the Holy Spirit with the evidence of speaking with other tongues. It would be power to do the works of Christ—to heal the sick, to preach the gospel, to see bondages of darkness broken, etc.

I say it often, and I will continue to say it: Every believer needs the baptism with the Holy Spirit, which, as already stated, is always accompanied by the speaking with other tongues as the Spirit of God gives the utterance (Acts 2:4). It doesn't matter who you are, you need the baptism with the Holy Spirit. If you are a schoolteacher, the Holy Spirit will help you to be a better teacher. If you are a plumber, the Holy Spirit will help you to be a better plumber. If you are a lawyer, the Holy Spirit will help you to be a better lawyer. If you are a truck driver, the Holy Spirit will help you to be a better truck driver. That's the power of which we speak, which is needed by every believer.

However, the power we have just addressed is not power to overcome sin. To be sure, the Holy Spirit is most definitely involved in the power we are about to mention now, but the sad fact is, millions of Christians have been baptized with the Holy Spirit and constantly speak in tongues, which they should, but still are not able to live a victorious life. That leaves one very confused.

Paul said, *"There is therefore now no condemnation to them which are in Christ Jesus, who walk not after the flesh but after the Spirit"* (Rom. 8:1). Paul is speaking of the Holy Spirit, and he is speaking of victory over sin.

That's what he also said when he made the statement: *"For the preaching of the Cross is to them who perish foolishness; but unto we who are saved it is the power of God"* (I Cor. 1:18).

Whereas he has been talking about power for service, he is now talking about power for victory over sin. They are two different things altogether.

Let me say it another way: There are millions of believers who are saved, Spirit-filled, and being used of God. They love the Lord. They aren't hypocrites, but they are struggling with the problem in their lives, which is sin, and they have not been able to gain the victory. They don't understand it. What are they doing wrong?

They have confused the two, service and victory over sin.

To have victory over sin, the believer must place his faith exclusively in Christ and the Cross, and maintain it exclusively in Christ and the Cross. With that being done, the Holy Spirit will greatly work with us and for us and give us victory over the world, the flesh, and the Devil. That is God's way.

Many Christians are trying to use the power that comes with the mighty baptism with the Holy Spirit that is intended for service to give them victory over sin. It won't work that way. It's so easy to place our faith in Christ and the Cross, which will then give the Holy Spirit the latitude to give us victory over sin in every capacity. No, the Scriptures do not teach sinless perfection, but they do teach that sin is not to have dominion over us (Rom. 6:14).

So, now you have the work of the Holy Spirit in the two parts in which He is engaged:

1. The Holy Spirit for service
2. The Holy Spirit giving us victory over sin and over the world, the flesh, and the Devil.

LET NOT SIN THEREFORE REIGN IN YOUR MORTAL BODY

"Let not sin therefore reign in your mortal body, that you should obey it in the lusts thereof" (Rom. 6:12).

The very fact that Paul tells us not to allow sin to rule in our mortal bodies presents the fact that it most definitely can do so. This means that the sin nature can rule the Christian and make life miserable to say the least. Unfortunately, many in the church world do not even believe that there is such a thing as a sin nature. What Paul actually said was, "Let not *the* sin," meaning that the definite article is in front of the word *sin.* This means that Paul is not speaking of acts of sin, but rather the sin nature.

All of this tells us that sin is not dead, and neither is the believer completely free from sin, even though he is free (or should be free) from its dominion.

The word *reign* in the Greek is *basileuo* and means "to exercise kingly power." Even though the sin nature is still in the believer's heart and life, it is supposed to be a dethroned monarch, so to speak. Consequently, the believer has the responsibility of keeping it from mounting the throne of his heart, for that is the place that the Lord Jesus alone should occupy. Please understand that the believer can only do that by understanding that Jesus Christ is the source of all things we receive from God.

As well, the Cross of Christ is the means, and the only means, by which these things are given to us. If the believer does not come to the place just mentioned, to be sure, the sin nature will most definitely rule and reign in one's mortal body.

THAT YOU SHOULD OBEY IT IN THE LUSTS THEREOF

The heading tells us emphatically that the sin nature is still present in the believer, but we do not have to obey it anymore, that is, if we understand the Cross of Christ.

Now, to what does the word *it* refer—to the sin nature or to the physical body?

Logic would lead us to relate this pronoun to the sin nature; however, the Greek text refers it back to the physical body. It is true that sinful desires originate with the evil nature, not with the physical body, but why does Paul relate them to the body in this instance?

The answer is found in the fact that the sinful nature is an intangible, invisible entity and, in fact, cannot be watched, as should be obvious. It is an unseen enemy whose tactics cannot be observed and, therefore, cannot be guarded against.

However, the saint is able to keep watch over the members of his physical body—what his eyes see, what his ears hear, what his mind thinks about, what his hands do, and where his feet carry him. Due to the divine nature in the believer, he now has the power to guide the actions of the physical body, which means exactly what Paul said—that he does not have to *"obey it in the lusts thereof."* Again we state, that is if he understands the Cross of Christ and places his faith accordingly.

In fact, it is through the physical body that Satan hooks the individual, so to speak. While sin definitely originates in the heart, it cannot be brought to full fruition unless the physical body is engaged in some way. Therefore, the believer finds that it is the physical body that is constantly giving him trouble respecting ungodly passions, etc. This is what Paul is talking about.

SINLESS PERFECTION?

I think it should be obvious from Romans 6:12 and related verses that sinless perfection is not possible in the heart and life of the believer at present. In fact, as stated, Paul is saying that the sin nature remains in the believer; however, it does not reign or have dominion anymore over the believer.

We say it again: The sin nature will not reign or have dominion if the believer places his or her faith exclusively in Christ and the Cross, and maintains it exclusively in Christ and the Cross. If that is not done, the sin nature is once again going to rule the believer.

Concerning sinless perfection, Paul said, *"For all have sinned, and come short of the glory of God"* (Rom. 3:23).

The coming short of the glory of God is not something that pertains only to the unbeliever as some think, but it pertains to the believer as well. It speaks of something that is taking place constantly and will continue to do so until the resurrection of life. In fact, any person who is close to God to any degree fully understands this. He realizes his shortcomings, flaws, and even occasional failures. It is not right, and the believer is not forced to do such, but, nevertheless, it happens.

THE DEGREE OF PERFECTION

In fact, the degree of perfection demanded by God is so far beyond our understanding of such that there is really no way to compare man's definition of perfection with that which God demands. In truth, the believer can only come up to that level in Christ; nevertheless, the Holy Spirit is constantly working with us in these areas. Also, even though all are constantly coming short of the glory of God, which includes even the godliest among us, at the same time, the blood of Jesus is constantly cleansing us from all sin (from coming short of His glory). In other words, the Lord is constantly making intercession for us (Heb. 7:25).

CONFESSION OF SIN

No, this does not mean that the Lord automatically forgives sin when it is committed by the believer. When sin is purposefully committed, it must be purposefully repented of before God (I Jn. 1:9).

The coming short of the glory simply pertains to our everyday life and living, without any purposeful acts of sin, be they overt or covert. As stated, if one is close to the Lord at all, this reality will quickly become obvious in one's life. Actually, that is one of the things Jesus said in what we refer to as the

Lord's Prayer: *"Forgive us our debts* (trespasses), *as we forgive our debtors* (those who trespass against us)*"* (Mat. 6:12). While this pertains to known sins committed, it also pertains to things of which we are not at times fully aware.

As we have stated several times in the past, the sin nature is allowed to remain in the believer as a disciplinary measure. To be sure, it works well. It helps the believer to understand that within himself, he is weak and unable to do what needs to be done, and he must constantly depend on Christ.

NEITHER YIELD YOU YOUR MEMBERS AS INSTRUMENTS OF UNRIGHTEOUSNESS UNTO SIN

"Neither yield you your members as instruments of unrighteousness unto sin: but yield yourselves unto God, as those who are alive from the dead, and your members as instruments of righteousness unto God" (Rom. 6:13).

In this verse, Paul is speaking of the physical body. It is neutral, meaning that it's neither righteous nor unrighteous. It is what we make of it. As we've already stated, while sin begins in the heart, it must be carried out in some way through the physical body. So, the great apostle tells us that we are to yield the members of our physical body to righteousness instead of unrighteousness.

Yet, if we attempt to do this by the means of willpower alone, it will not be done. While the will is most definitely important (*"whosoever will"*) still, within itself, it is not powerful enough to overcome sin in that fashion.

Unfortunately, all too many preachers teach that when a person gives his heart to Christ, the Lord then gives him some type of super willpower to where he can say no to the Devil. That is not scriptural. As we've already stated, while the will is important, as should be overly obvious, it is effective only in the choices we make as it regards obeying the Lord or disobeying Him. What do we mean by that? The believer has the choice of accepting Christ and the Cross or accepting something else. That's where the choice begins and ends. So, the believer can yield the members of his physical body to righteousness only if his faith is exclusively in Christ and the Cross. Only then will the Holy Spirit help such a believer, and this we must ever understand.

BUT YIELD YOURSELVES UNTO GOD

The heading refers to yielding one's will to God. As stated, the believer now has the power to do this. In Christ, He can yield or not yield, that is, if he follows God's prescribed order, which we will give momentarily. If he tries to do it solely by the will, he will fail.

IS IT POSSIBLE FOR SATAN TO FORCE THE WILL OF A BELIEVER?

Yes, contrary to the beliefs of most Christians, Satan can override the will of a Christian and force the Christian to do something he does not want to do and, in fact, is fighting with all of his strength not to do. This is true providing the Christian does not follow the path laid out by the Lord. Some would then say that if a person is forced against his will, he is not responsible.

Oh, yes, he is!

To be frank, the area that the will is most important—and it definitely is important—is that we say yes to Christ or no to Christ. That's where the will begins and ends. If we say no to Christ, then we have just opened the door for Satan to force us into a position that we do not desire to be.

What we have just stated flies in the face of most teaching, and to be sure, it is a frightening prospect (Rom. 7:18).

If this is so, and it is, we certainly want to know the safeguards against such action, especially considering how so very important all of this is. In fact, this situation is a part of every believer, and if we do not know God's way, we are going to buy ourselves some trouble.

HOW CAN SATAN DO SUCH A THING?

First of all (to which we have already eluded), if the believer steps outside of the prescribed path laid down by the Lord (which most do at times), then the believer is left with nothing but his willpower to overcome Satan, which is always woefully inadequate. In other words, irrespective of how strong the will of a Christian may be, within itself, it is no match for Satan.

Paul said it very dogmatically in Romans 7:15: *"For that which I do I allow not* (should have been translated, 'I understand not'):

for what I would (desire to do, the will), *that do I not; but what I hate* (to fail the Lord), *that do I.*"

No, this is not the account of Paul before his conversion, but rather after his conversion. It was even after being baptized with the Holy Spirit and after beginning to preach the gospel. The truth is that while the unsaved may hate the results of sin, they do not hate sin. In fact, they love sin, which is the reason many sinners do not want to give their hearts to Christ. They simply do not want to give up their sins. So, this statement, as well as others in Romans, Chapter 7, proclaims the experience of the apostle in trying with all of his strength to do that which was right, but failing.

HOW DO I DO IT?

As well, in Romans, Chapter 7, Paul directly addressed the will of man and its inadequacy by saying, *"For to will is present with me; but how to perform that which is good I find not"* (Rom. 7:18).

So, Paul is here plainly stating that the will is not strong enough within itself to overcome Satan.

He also told us in his epistle to the Galatians how to live the overcoming life. He then made the statement, *"I do not frustrate the grace of God,"* simply meaning that it is possible to do such a thing (Gal. 2:20-21). If the believer does not have his faith exclusively in Christ and the Cross, such a believer is definitely frustrating the grace of God, which puts such a person in a precarious situation.

The idea is this: If we do not follow the Lord's prescribed order of victory, we will definitely frustrate the grace of God. This means that God's grace cannot function within us to bring about the holiness required if we, at the same time, are attempting to do so within our own strength. Our own personal efforts in the wrong direction cancel out the grace of God, which invites Satan to ply his wares, making it impossible for us to obey.

The Christian can only do what is right by the enabling grace of God, and if that is lacking, he fails, irrespective of how hard he is trying to do otherwise.

HINDRANCES

The problem is self-will, which translates into the flesh. In other words, we are attempting to solve the problem in our own strength. What makes this thing so subtle is that most of the time, we think that our efforts in the flesh are really in the Spirit when they aren't. Especially considering how religious our personal efforts are, we are easily fooled it seems.

The simple truth is that if we follow God's glorious prescribed methods, paid for by Jesus Christ and freely given unto any and all believers, we cannot fail. That way is the Cross. If we follow other methods, irrespective of how well meaning and sincere we may be, we cannot help but fail.

One must consider that if this problem is so severe (and severe it is) that Jesus had to die on Calvary in our place and be resurrected from the dead, then we should realize that there is

simply no other way for this great thing to be brought about—
this continuous victory within our hearts and lives—except by
that which He has done for us.

GOD'S PRESCRIBED ORDER OF VICTORY

We have given the following already in this volume, but
because of its great significance, please allow the repetition.
The following is God's prescribed order of victory in brief form:

- Jesus Christ is the source of all things we receive from
  God (Jn. 1:1-3, 14, 29; 14:6)
- While Jesus is the source, the Cross of Christ is the
  means, and the only means, by which all of these wonderful things are given to us (I Cor. 1:17-18, 23; 2:2;
  Col. 2:10-15)
- If Jesus is the source and the Cross is the means, then
  the Cross of Christ must be the object of our faith. In
  fact, the story of Jesus Christ and Him crucified is
  the entirety of the story of the Bible (Rom. 6:1-5, 12;
  Col. 2:10-15)
- With Jesus as our source and the Cross as our means, and
  the Cross of Christ ever the object of our faith, the Holy
  Spirit, who works exclusively within the parameters of
  the Cross, which gives Him the legal means, will then
  work mightily on our behalf. This is God's prescribed
  order. He does not work any other way because no other
  way is needed. It is always the Cross, the Cross, the
  Cross! (Rom. 8:1-11; Eph. 2:13-18; Acts 1:4; Gal. 6:14)

AS THOSE WHO ARE ALIVE FROM THE DEAD

The heading refers to believers who were dead to God before their conversion. Consequently, they had no power to yield the members of their physical bodies to that which is right, but rather were at the mercy of Satan. He has no mercy. Now, after coming to Christ, they have the power of the sin nature broken, with the divine nature imparted. The believer is now *alive*, in the sense of being alive unto God, and has the power to do what he once could not do, that is, if he follows God's prescribed order to yield unto God.

AND YOUR MEMBERS AS INSTRUMENTS OF RIGHTEOUSNESS UNTO GOD

The heading proclaims this power now available to the believer, but only as he knows and understands what Jesus has done for him in breaking the dominion of sin in his life. Irrespective of Satan's power—and he does have power—the believer can now yield himself as he should, and there is nothing that Satan can do.

As I trust we have properly explained, when Paul speaks of *"your members,"* he is speaking of our physical bodies—our eyes, ears, tongue, feet, hands—in fact, every member of our physical bodies. As previously stated, this is so important because it is in the physical body that Satan causes us problems. Sin actually begins, as stated, in the heart, which, in reality, is the soul and the spirit, but it plays out in the physical body. In actuality, it cannot come to fruition except through body members. This is where every evil impulse is carried out.

However, the believer now has the power to do the very opposite with the members of his physical body—to yield to righteousness—but only if he follows God's prescribed order that we have just given, which, in effect, is the Cross.

Amazing grace! How sweet the sound
That saved a wretch like me!
I once was lost, but now am found;
Was blind, but now I see.

CHAPTER 10

DOMINION

DOMINION

"FOR SIN SHALL NOT have dominion over you: for you are not under the law, but under grace" (Rom. 6:14).

FOR SIN SHALL NOT HAVE DOMINION OVER YOU

The heading tells us that sin is still alive and as powerful as ever, but it is not a danger to the child of God who follows the prescribed pattern laid out by the Holy Spirit.

The dominion of sin is broken respecting the child of God. Actually, this happens at the very moment the person comes to Christ; however, to maintain this victory, the believer must understand what Christ has done for him in this respect. He must, as well, have faith that the Holy Spirit will energize this great truth in his life.

The statement, as given by the Holy Spirit through the apostle, is dogmatic in that it is impossible for sin to have dominion over the believer as long as the believer is abiding by the Word of God. The saint should live his life every day with the consciousness of that fact in his mind.

WHAT IS DOMINION?

The Greek word for dominion is *kurieuo* and means "to rule, to be lord of, to exercise lordship over." In other words, it is a powerful force, in fact, more powerful than the person can withstand, at least within himself. When the sin nature is dominating the life of a believer, such a person will not be able to throw over the compulsion as it regards the sin, whatever it might be. It doesn't matter if that believer is Spirit-filled and is even being mightily used of God, which does happen. The Cross of Christ is the only answer for the sin question. There is no other as there need be no other.

The sad fact is that 90 percent (and I think I exaggerate not) of the modern church is dominated by the sin nature, meaning that sin has dominion over them in some way. I'm speaking of those who truly love the Lord!

HOW CAN I SAY THAT?

How do I know that? Ninety percent is an appalling figure. Yes, it is, but it is true.

Let me explain: The modern church understands the Cross of Christ as it regards salvation but not at all as it regards sanctification. So, to be blunt, that means that modern Christians simply do not know how to live for God. As a result, they try to do for themselves what only the Holy Spirit can do. Once again, I'm speaking of those who truly love the Lord.

Because this is so important, please allow me to repeat myself: The modern church has no understanding at all as it regards the Cross of Christ respecting sanctification.

Salvation, yes.

Sanctification, no.

As a result, sin dominates such a person, and please believe me, this is not a pleasant experience.

However, this is not the way that it's supposed to be. The Lord has given us the means of victory, and that means is the Cross of Christ, which we've already explained a few paragraphs back.

FOR YOU ARE NOT UNDER THE LAW, BUT UNDER GRACE

Every person in the world, and I mean every person, is under either law or grace. Every unbeliever in the world, no matter his or her religious affiliation, if any at all, is under law. They don't know that, and they don't understand that, but it is true. One day, unless they come to Christ, they will have to answer to God for that broken law. The sad fact is that most believers are under law, as well, when the great apostle here emphatically tells us that this is not where the believer is to be.

Jesus satisfied the law in totality, and we speak of the law of Moses at Calvary's Cross.

Paul wrote: *"Christ has redeemed us from the curse of the law, being made a curse for us: for it is written, Cursed is everyone who hangs on a tree: that the blessing of Abraham might come on the Gentiles through Jesus Christ; that we might receive the promise of the Spirit through faith"* (Gal. 3:13-14).

So, if Jesus satisfied the law in every respect by living perfectly and dying as a sacrifice, why is it that virtually the entirety of the modern church is still under law? They are under law simply because they do not understand the Cross of Christ respecting sanctification. In other words, they don't understand how we live for God on a daily basis, how we order our behavior, and how we have victory over the world, the flesh, and the Devil. Not understanding that, they resort to law to try to live right. In fact, the church as a whole lurches from one fad to the other, and all is without any success.

WHAT DID PAUL MEAN BY US NOT BEING UNDER LAW BUT RATHER UNDER GRACE?

The law of Moses (or even laws we devise ourselves) tells us what to do or what not to do, but it doesn't really tell us how to do it. Law gives direction, but it gives no power whatsoever to the individual to keep the law. That's where the great problem is.

Grace does the opposite. We must understand that the grace of God comes through the Cross, in other words, is made possible by the Cross. Then, we must place our faith in the Cross of Christ, and maintain it in the Cross of Christ. When we do, the Holy Spirit, who works entirely within the framework of the finished work of Christ, will grandly help us.

He will not help us to try to keep the law. Now, think about that statement for a moment.

We can't get anything done without the Holy Spirit. It is for certain that the Holy Spirit will not help a believer try to keep the law, whether the law of Moses or laws we devise ourselves.

The reason is that Jesus Christ has already paid the price at Calvary's Cross in order that we may live the life we ought to live. For the Holy Spirit to try to help us keep some type of law is an insult to Christ. In essence, it is saying that what Christ did is not enough, and we have to add to it, whatever it is we can add. If you think about it a little bit, this is a gross insult, and it becomes understandable as to why the Holy Spirit won't help us try to keep laws.

The Holy Spirit wants your faith to be exclusively in Christ and the Cross. It should be obvious as to why—Jesus paid a great price at Calvary's Cross. There He atoned for all sin, and there He defeated every power of darkness, including all demon spirits, fallen angels, and Satan himself. So, for us to ignore that and try to do for ourselves what we can't do, and which Christ has already done is an insult of gross magnitude.

Let me give you an example or two of the way that we insult Christ. I am not saying that the perpetrator of such intends to do so, but that's what happens.

THE BOOK

Sometime back, Frances gave me a copy of the book, *The Purpose Driven Life*. She asked me to read it and tell her what

I thought about it. I read a few pages, laid it down, and didn't pick it back up. She asked me a little later as to my thoughts respecting the book.

"The man is trying to tell people how to live for God outside of the Cross of Christ, which means the book is of no worth at all." That is the truth.

Even though some 20 million copies were sold, I am told, still, the book really was law. Yet, the church bought into it hook, line, and sinker.

Let me say it again: There is victory over sin only in the Cross of Christ. We obtain that victory by evidencing faith in Christ and what He did for us at the Cross, and doing so on a perpetual basis.

So, Paul tells us that we are not under the law but that we're under grace, all because of what Jesus did for us at the Cross of Calvary. Yet, most believers do not understand that and continue placing their faith in something other than the Cross.

Jesus lived a life of perfection. He was the only one who ever did. He never sinned one single time in word, thought, or deed, and He did this as our representative man. In other words, He did it all for us. Our acceptance of Him pulls us from the position of lawbreaker to the position of law keeper, but only according to our faith in Him and what He did for us at the Cross.

Then, to address the broken law, of which all are guilty, Jesus offered up His perfect body as a sacrifice on Calvary's Cross. This addressed the problem that was incumbent upon every human being, for all had broken the law. However, acceptance of Him and what He has done for us wipes the slate clean, so to speak. This means that the law no longer points an accusing finger at us, at least if we function under grace and not law.

LAW

Paul is speaking of the law of Moses because that law is the crown prince of all laws simply because it was given by God and was, consequently, perfect. However, it also refers to any type of law (whatever it might be) that the believer devises, or even laws the churches devise for that matter, with the intention of bringing about a righteous life.

The idea is this: Whenever the believer faces sin and fails, if he does not properly know the Word of God, he will almost automatically institute a series of laws of his own making, or the making of someone else. He thinks that by keeping these laws, he will have victory. In other words, he will pray so much each day, read so many Scriptures each day, witness to so many people about Christ, or fast so many days. The list is almost endless, and it's all to no avail.

LET ME GIVE YOU AN EXAMPLE

As previously mentioned, sometime back, Donnie told me that he had picked up a book written by a prominent Pentecostal preacher. Please understand that I do not doubt the sincerity of the young man, but his direction is totally wrong.

In the book he stated, and I paraphrase from memory, "If you want victory over sin, fast 21 days," or words to that effect.

Fasting is definitely scriptural, that is, if done correctly, but fasting will not give anyone victory over sin. If it did, all that Jesus had to do was tell people to fast, and Calvary would have been unnecessary; however, we know that was not the case.

Yet, the church falls for this, thinking this is the answer and the solution, but it isn't.

LET ME GIVE ANOTHER EXAMPLE

I received a letter sometime back from a dear brother with whom I was not acquainted. He had been to a seminar, with the object in mind of having victory over sin. It was for preachers and their wives only.

In fact, I am acquainted with the man who originated these types of meetings. At any rate, he had bought into this fad with great delight.

All the preachers and their wives were instructed to bring a pad and a pencil, and then after the host had spoken for a short period of time, they were told to write all their sins down on their pads.

They were all then to stand and face each other, with a man facing a man and a woman facing a woman, and read these sins out loud for all to hear. The brother in question was quick to state that his sins were not nearly as bad as many others. Then, when this was completed, they were to tear out of the pad the sheet of paper containing the list of sins. Then they were to tear the sheet into many pieces. They were then to hold their hands high with all the pieces of paper and open their hands and let the paper flutter to the floor. Now comes the crowning act of all.

WHATSOEVER IS NOT OF FAITH IS SIN

They were to jump up and down on top of the pieces of paper, shouting their victory now that sin no longer had dominion over them.

It would be funny if it weren't so sad.

Is such a thing as this scriptural?

No!

Not only is it not scriptural, it's silly! Yet, as stated, the church lurches from one fad to the other.

In fact, any effort that we make to have victory in this walk of life, other than the Cross of Christ and our faith in that finished work, is constituted by the Lord as sin.

Paul said so: *"For whatsoever is not of faith is sin"* (Rom. 14:23).

So, individuals who bought the book, *The Purpose Driven Life,* and read it with the intention of getting victory over sin were actually sinning by doing so. The same could be said for the fasting and the tearing up of the pieces of paper containing the list of sins. As stated, and we say it again: it's one fad after another.

WHAT'S WRONG WITH THE CROSS?

All these things mentioned have been turned into law. Fasting is not law, but we make it a law by claiming that it is meant to do something that God never intended. Law cannot set anyone free. Even the law of Moses never effected any type of salvation or victory for anyone. It was not designed by God for that purpose or intended to be used in that fashion. It was very valuable for that which it was intended, but only for that which it was intended. By doing these things, even as good as some of them may be, we are at the same time saying that what Jesus did at the Cross is not enough. In other words, it needs our contribution to make it effective. While we may not mean it in that fashion, such thinking is an insult to the finished work of Christ.

To be sure, Jesus paid the full price for sin, and, as well, He paid the full price that sin may not have dominion over us.

THERE IS NO SUCH THING AS MORAL EVOLUTION

Even though we have addressed this thought previously, it is so important, please allow our repetition.

There was a time that baseball was America's pastime, but now self-improvement is America's greatest pastime. The sad fact is, there are billions of dollars spent in this regard, but of all the fads men try (and the gurus who promise such are multitudinous), still, there is no help in this sector whatsoever.

What is moral evolution?

It's simply the idea that we can improve ourselves outside of the Lord. While all of us most definitely need improvement, it can only be gained in one way, and that is by the believer placing his or her faith exclusively in Christ and the Cross, and maintaining it in Christ and the Cross exclusively (I Cor. 1:17-18, 23; 2:2; Gal. 6:14; Rom. 8:2; Phil. 3:17-19; Col. 2:10-15).

Despite the fact that there is never any help from this source, preachers (and they are a dime a dozen) who specialize in moral evolution have the biggest crowds ever.

While man definitely needs improvement, in many ways, there is only one way that this improvement can take place, and it has worked in the hearts and lives of untold millions down through the many centuries. That is for the believer to place his or her faith exclusively in Christ and the Cross.

WHY DO BELIEVERS RESORT TO LAW OR SELF-EFFORT SO OFTEN?

First of all, there is something in man, even godly believers, that wants to do something to effect our salvation or victory. It is a bleed-over from the fall. Sinner man thinks he is self-sufficient, with him never realizing that his biggest problem is a failure to humble himself before God. As stated, this carries over into the believer as well. Somehow it makes us feel good to think that we have contributed something toward whatever it is that we are seeking, even though, in reality, we have actually contributed nothing. In fact, we are hindering what the Lord has already done. It appeals to us because it addresses itself to our ego. It ministers to our self-importance, and we like that.

Yet, we still continue to try to bring about these qualities and attributes in our hearts and lives by whatever methods are at our disposal. This makes us feel very religious and very worthy when, in reality, all we have done is hinder the grace of God in our lives.

Secondly, many believers attempt to do for themselves what, in reality, Christ has already done. Most of the time, it is simply because of an ignorance of the Scriptures. They simply do not know what the Word of God says about the matter.

To be frank, I do not recall in all of my life ever hearing a sermon preached respecting the subject we are presently engaging. Now, I am certain that it has been preached sometime in the past by some preachers, but not often respecting the totality of the church.

WHY?

If the message is not preached, the people do not hear or know. I believe that the main reason it is not preached is simply because most preachers do not know or realize (even as we have already said) that what Jesus did at Calvary and the resurrection was, in effect, a double cure.

He paid the sin debt, and He also broke the power of sin over the lives of believers. While the Bible does not teach sinless perfection, it most definitely does teach, even as we are now studying, that sin is not to have dominion over us. What Jesus did was a twofold work. He paid the price for our salvation, and He also paid the price for our victory on a daily basis (Lk. 9:23).

The gist of what Paul is saying in Romans 6:14 is that if we attempt to gain victory under law, the sin nature will definitely have dominion over us; however, if we understand what Christ did, then the sin bondage will be forever broken. Of course, that means that we must understand that it was for us and that, in effect, we were in Him when He did these great things. As well, we must accept all that He did by faith, which guarantees us the grace of God, which is the goodness of God extended to undeserving saints.

WHAT THEN?

"What then? shall we sin, because we are not under the law, but under grace? God forbid" (Rom. 6:15).

The short question, *"What then?"* presents Paul going back to the first question he asked in this chapter, *"Shall we continue in sin, that grace may abound?"*

Due to the fact that the carnal mind (especially the carnal religious mind) will read it wrong, Paul addresses the subject again because it is so very important.

The whole idea is, as it regards believers, what are we going to do about sin? Well, Paul gives us the answer in Romans, Chapter 6. It is given in proverbial black and white.

He first of all takes us straight to the Cross (Rom. 6:1-5). That and that alone is the solution—it is the Cross! The Cross! The Cross!

Some say that we make too much of the Cross. One brother wrote me the other day and said, "Why do you keep talking about the Cross? We already know all about that." The truth is that he did not know anything about the Cross, or at least precious little. Believe it or not, that's the condition of the modern church. It knows nothing about the Cross of Christ relative to our sanctification.

SHALL WE SIN BECAUSE WE ARE NOT UNDER THE LAW BUT UNDER GRACE?

Some believers in Paul's time were reading wrong that which he had said about grace. "If grace was so powerful, even greater than sin, why be worried about sin," seemed to be their attitude.

The greatest hindrance to faith is sin. It weakens the faith of the individual. I remember years ago hearing the great preacher A. N. Trotter make the following statement: "Every attack by Satan, irrespective of the direction that it might take, is but for one purpose, and that is to destroy our faith, or at least seriously weaken it."

Sin does that! It weakens our faith. Please understand that our entire walk with God, and I mean everything, is hinged on our faith. For it to be faith that is proper, it must be faith in Christ and what Christ has done for us at the Cross. Nothing else will be accepted by God.

Just because grace is greater than sin, and it most definitely is, it doesn't mean that we should look at sin with impunity. That's like looking at the bite of a rattlesnake as not so bad simply because there is a serum that will counteract it. Such thinking is stupid to say the least!

To be frank, anytime that we take sin lightly, we are functioning in the arena of stupidity. We must never forget that Jesus

Christ did not save us in sin, but rather from sin. As we have already said several times, the Bible does not teach sinless perfection, for such is not possible with the believer, at least at this time. However, it most definitely does teach that sin is not to have dominion over us.

Every true believer hates sin. Sometimes the flesh may want something that's wrong, but the inner man doesn't. Anytime we fail the Lord in any capacity, it is like a blow to our spirit, which it definitely is. Every believer knows exactly what I'm talking about.

GOD FORBID

Paul answered the question of continuing sin in the heart and life of the believer with the following: *"God forbid."* Those two words were Paul's answer to the problem of continued sin.

Grace is never a license to sin, but rather the very opposite. Actually, it is liberty to live a holy life.

Is God's grace a condoning of sin?

No!

Does God's grace make sin inconsequential, in other words, insignificant?

Again, God forbid, no!

Grace is simply the goodness of God extended to undeserving people. The Cross of Christ has made grace possible to a degree never known before. That's the reason that our faith must ever be anchored in Christ and the Cross. It was there that every sin was atoned. It was there that eternal mercy was forever granted. Just because God will forgive sin upon proper confession, that doesn't make sin any less lethal. The believer must understand that.

DO YOU NOT KNOW...?

"Know you not, that to whom you yield yourselves servants to obey, his servants you are to whom you obey; whether of sin unto death, or of obedience unto righteousness?" (Rom. 6:16).

The question of our heading presents Paul answering the question even to a greater degree by showing that the believer has changed masters.

The word *servants* in the Greek text is *doulos* and means "the most abject, servile term for a slave in the Greek language." So, instead of being translated "servants," it should have been translated "slaves."

The believer was a slave of Satan before salvation, but since he has been saved, he is now a slave of the Lord Jesus Christ. However, being a slave of Jesus Christ is altogether different than being a slave of Satan.

Concerning this, Jesus said:

Come unto Me (is meant by Jesus to reveal Himself as the giver of salvation), *all you who labor and are heavy laden* (trying to earn salvation by works), *and I will give you rest* (this 'rest' can only be found by placing one's faith in Christ and what He has done for us at the Cross [Gal. 5:1-6]). *Take My yoke upon you* (the 'yoke' of the 'Cross' [Lk. 9:23]), *and learn of Me* (learn of His sacrifice [Rom. 6:3-5]); *for I am meek and lowly in heart* (the only thing that our Lord person- ally said of Himself): *and you shall find rest unto your souls* (the soul can find rest only in Christ). *For My yoke is easy, and My burden is light* (what He requires of us is very little, just to have faith in Him and His sacrificial atoning work) (Mat. 11:28-30) (The Expositor's Study Bible).

Now, with Satan, it's another matter altogether.

A SLAVE OF SATAN

The word *doulos* refers to one who is born into a condition of slavery. We inherited a totally depraved nature from our parents through Adam—a nature that made us love sin and compelled us to serve it habitually.

There is pleasure in sin for a season (Heb. 11:25), but it quickly degenerates into bondage, which makes life hell on earth. Tragi- cally and sadly, that is the condition of most of the human race. There are 40 million alcoholics in America and some 20 million problem drinkers. Now, I don't really know the difference between an alcoholic and a problem drinker, but those are the statistics.

There are nearly 40 million who are bound by drugs of one nature or another. Then, if we lay these vices aside, untold mil- lions are bound in a prison of fear, hatred, or unforgiveness, with religion probably being the greatest bondage of all.

The reason for so much alcoholism and drug addiction is because people try to face life without God, which they cannot do. So they seek for something that will calm the hurt, the guilt, and the condemnation, even for a short period of time. As stated, it soon becomes a terrible bondage, which makes them slaves of Satan.

IN THE WILL OF GOD

Again, the word *doulos* means "one whose will is swallowed up in the will of another."

Paul argues that before salvation, the person's will was swallowed up in the will of Satan, but since he has been saved, his will is swallowed up in the sweet will of God. Since that is so, he does not desire to live a life of occasional sin. In other words, he takes sin very seriously and never passes it off lightly.

BOUND TO ANOTHER

Again, the word *doulos* refers to one who is bound to another in bands so strong that only death can break them. The believer's identification with the Lord Jesus in His death broke the bands that bound him to Satan. Now he is bound to the Lord Jesus as His bondslave in bands so strong that only death can break them, and, actually, death will not break these bonds.

Since Christ is the believer's life, and He (Jesus) will never die again, the believer is bound to Him forever. The only way he could live a life of planned sin is to become again the slave of the evil nature and Satan. This the believer will do if his faith is placed in anything except Christ and the Cross, and, as well, it must be maintained in Christ and the Cross. Just because the believer does this and is proficient in his effort, still, Satan will not give up easily. We must understand that. Unfortunately, many believers think that once they understand the Cross to a certain degree, then Satan will not bother them anymore. That's not going to happen! You are going to have Satan and his cohorts of darkness to contend with until the trump sounds or God calls you home.

Despite our faith being in the right place and maintained in the right place, which means according to the Word of God, sometimes the believer will still fail. I should say this is a fact. The believer must understand that no matter how difficult at times the journey might be, there is no other way than Christ and the Cross. We must understand that, know that, and fashion our lives accordingly. It is Jesus Christ and Him crucified, which means there is nothing else.

IN DISREGARD OF HIS OWN INTERESTS

The word *doulos* also means "one who serves another to the disregard of his own interests." The sinner serves Satan to the disregard of his own best interests. He does so because he is compelled to do so. He is a slave. For his trouble, he gets sin and death and sorrow and suffering.

The believer, with his own will and accord, serves the Lord Jesus with an abandon that says, "Nothing matters about me, just as long as the Lord Jesus is glorified."

Of course, a person who disregards himself for the sake of the Lord Jesus does not want to live a life of sin in any form, and to be sure, will experience more abundant life, which Satan cannot give.

WHETHER OF SIN UNTO DEATH, OR OF OBEDIENCE UNTO RIGHTEOUSNESS?

The heading presents two masters here contrasted—sin and righteousness. A man must be the servant of one or the other, for no man can serve two masters.

So, the believer has it laid out before him. He can choose the path other than the Cross, which will lead to sin unto death, or he can choose the Cross, which will be obedience unto righteousness, which is joy unspeakable and full of glory. However, please understand that the only way the believer can walk in victory, and I mean the only way, is for the believer's faith to be placed entirely in Christ and what Christ has done for us at the Cross, and maintained in that posture forever.

BUT GOD BE THANKED, THAT YOU WERE THE SERVANTS OF SIN

"But God be thanked, that you were the servants of sin, but you have obeyed from the heart that form of doctrine which was delivered you" (Rom. 6:17).

The heading speaks of a past tense. In other words, the believer is no more a slave of sin because of what Paul said in the next phrase. Actually, the phrase has two meanings.

First of all, it speaks of what the individuals were before conversion (before coming to Christ). They were servants of sin, meaning slaves to sin in every form, which is the condition of all unbelievers.

It also pertains to believers who had placed their faith in something other than Christ and the Cross, and once again, sadly enough, became a slave of sin all over again. However, they heard Paul teach the truth of the Cross, and they placed their faith therein and began to walk in victory as God intended.

Paul said, *"But you have obeyed from the heart that form of doctrine that was delivered you."*

To better explain this statement by Paul, the word *delivered* in the Greek text is somewhat different than normally used. Consequently, it would have been better translated "the form of doctrine into which you were delivered." While it is true that the doctrines of salvation were delivered to us, and we, by the grace of God, believed them, that is not what Paul is saying here in the Greek. He is actually saying that the believer was delivered into the form of doctrine, that is, the Message of the Cross one might say.

First of all, to have that for which Jesus has paid such a price, there must be obedience from the heart. In fact, we find that most who reject the Message of the Cross do so because of unbelief. They simply don't believe that what Jesus did at the Cross answers every question and, in reality, solves every problem. In other words, they have placed their faith in something else. For us to have that which Jesus paid such a price, there must be obedience from the heart, and that means that it is more than a mental acceptance. In fact, it goes back to the previous verse where Paul talks about us becoming a slave of Christ.

That's the reason that many believers never receive the tremendous benefits of the Cross. It is because their consecration has been tepid, to say the least. They have not obeyed from the heart, but rather have given only a mental affirmation, if even that.

To properly obey means that one has given up all other approaches and all other efforts, irrespective of what they might be. Now, this somewhat presents a problem.

This is where the *"offense of the Cross"* comes in (Gal. 5:11). When our faith is in the Cross of Christ, God gets the glory for anything and everything that is done, which, of course, is proper and right. Whenever something is done through the means of the flesh, and that means anything other than the Cross of Christ, man gets the glory, which God cannot tolerate. This is where obedience comes in. Do we do it God's way, or do we do it man's way?

THAT FORM OF DOCTRINE

The Greek word for *form* is *tupos* and means a "stamp, a shape, a model, a pattern."

In essence, a form constitutes the foundation of a house, and it constitutes the foundation of the gospel at present.

The Cross of Christ is actually the foundation of all doctrine. In other words, every Bible doctrine is built on the foundation of the Cross. Whenever error is brought about, it's always when the Cross of Christ is ignored, misunderstood, or outright rejected. In fact, the Cross was the first doctrine formulated in the mind of the Godhead as it regarded the redemption of humanity.

God, through foreknowledge, knew He would create the universe, He would create this planet called Earth, and that He would create man. He also knew that man would fall (I Pet. 1:20).

BEFORE THE FOUNDATION OF THE WORLD

It was determined by the Godhead, even before the foundation of the world, that man would be redeemed by God becoming man and giving Himself as a sacrifice on the Cross, hence, the Holy Spirit through Peter saying:

Forasmuch as you know that you were not redeemed with corruptible things, as silver and gold, from your vain conversation (vain lifestyle) *received by tradition from your fathers* (speaks of original sin that is passed on from father to child at conception); *but with the precious blood of Christ* (presents the payment, which proclaims the poured out life of Christ on behalf of sinners), *as of a Lamb without blemish and without spot* (speaks of the lambs offered as substitutes in the old Jewish economy; the death of Christ was not an execution or assassination, but rather a sacrifice; the offering of Himself presented a perfect sacrifice, for He was perfect in every respect [Ex. 12:5]): *who verily was foreordained before the foundation of the world, but was manifest in these last times for you* (I Pet. 1:18-20).

When a house is laid out to be constructed, it might be said that the form is the single most important thing simply because it guarantees the foundation. If the form is wrong, then everything else is going to be wrong. If the form is right, everything else is going to be right.

The form of the gospel is right—it is the Cross of Christ.

DELIVERED

As we've already stated, the word *delivered*, as Paul uses it here, is different than is normally used. It refers to the foundation of the Cross given to the body of Christ, in reality, the new covenant. In fact, Jesus Christ is the new covenant, and the Cross of Christ is the meaning of that covenant—the meaning of which was given to the apostle Paul (Gal. 1:1-12). If it has been changed, and it has in most circles, it's man who changed it and not God. The new covenant was delivered to us by and through the Cross of Christ.

To say it another way: The manner in which the Holy Spirit has described this finished work of Christ to the believer makes it impossible for the believer to fail, that is, if the believer obeys the Word. As stated, all it takes is knowing and understanding what's been done and having faith in what has been done. Considering that the Holy Spirit will help us to do both, none of us has any excuse.

BEING THEN MADE FREE FROM SIN

"Being then made free from sin, you became the servants of righteousness" (Rom. 6:18).

The heading actually means that we are now free from the sin nature in that it has no more power over us.

How was that brought about?

It was brought about totally and completely by the Cross of Christ and our faith in that finished work. That is the solution and the answer for every problem that plagues the human race—the Cross of Christ. As we have just stated, Jesus Christ is the new covenant, but the Cross of Christ is literally the meaning of the new covenant.

Paul actually said, "Being made free from the sin," meaning that he is not speaking of acts of sin, but rather the sin nature.

YOU BECAME THE SERVANTS OF RIGHTEOUSNESS

Once again Paul uses the definite article in front of the word *righteousness,* making it say "*the* righteousness."

He is speaking of the righteousness imputed by God to the believing sinner, which is freely given.

There is only one way this righteousness of God can be bestowed upon anyone, and that is according to his faith in Christ and what He did for us at the Cross.

That being done institutes a pure, spotless righteousness, as stated, the righteousness of God instantly given to the believing sinner.

Paul is actually saying that having been set free from the evil nature and the slave to that nature, the believer is now constituted a slave of righteousness.

Being a slave of Christ is totally unlike the use of the word in any other capacity. While the meaning of the word is the same respecting Christ, the actual condition is altogether different, actually, such a difference that it is impossible to even compare such.

To serve Christ is a pleasure. To give one's very life to and for Him is a privilege. He is so good to the believer, so generous, so kind, and so literally giving of Himself that once one has served Him for any length of time, one delights in being His slave. To be frank, I would a thousand times rather be His slave than Satan's king.

Is there a heart that is waiting,
Longing for pardon today?
Hear the glad message we bring you,
Jesus is passing this way.

Coming in love and in mercy,
Quickly now unto Him go;
Open your heart to receive Him,
Pardon and peace He'll bestow.

Listen, the Spirit is calling
Jesus will freely forgive,
Why not this moment accept Him?
Trust in God's mercy and live.

He is so tender and loving,
He is so near you today;
Open your heart to receive Him,
While He is passing this way.

CHAPTER 11

RIGHTEOUSNESS

RIGHTEOUSNESS

"I SPEAK AFTER THE MANNER of men because of the infirmity of your flesh: for as you have yielded your members servants to uncleanness and to iniquity unto iniquity; even so now yield your members servants to righteousness unto holiness" (Rom. 6:19).

THE INFIRMITY OF YOUR FLESH

The heading actually has Paul apologizing in a sense for using the illustration drawn from human relations—that of a slave. However, he says that he was forced to do so because of the frailties of the flesh.

The idea is that these Romans, to whom he was writing, plus all of the human family for all time, had been slaves to the passions of sin before their conversion. With the flesh being what it is, it is very quickly enslaved to evil passions, and I speak of alcohol, drugs, gambling, lust, hate, anger, greed, jealousy, etc.

The flesh, as Paul uses the word, speaks of that which is indicative of a human being, such as his or her education, motivation, talent, ability, personal strength, etc. Most of these things aren't wrong within themselves, but the idea is that due to being weakened by the fall, man simply cannot live for God by means of the flesh. It cannot be done. That's the reason that if we go in any other way than God's way, which is the Cross of Christ, we will fail as fail we must.

SERVANTS TO UNCLEANLINESS

The heading details the lives of all believers before coming to Christ. Uncleanliness speaks of moral impurity, which plagues the human race. This is the very opposite of righteousness, which speaks of moral perfection, and which only God has and can give.

The manner in which Paul uses the phrase, *"And to iniquity unto iniquity,"* speaks of the destructive power of sin. In other words, one iniquity leads to another, consequently, making it impossible for one to break out of such a bondage, at least within his own capabilities. It just cannot be! Only the power of God can set the captive free.

A proper illustration would be that of quicksand. The more a person struggles in that mixture, the more it tends to have the very opposite effect of what's desired. The person actually gets deeper into the quagmire, and thus is sin. That is why David said, *"I waited patiently for the Lord; and He inclined unto me, and heard my cry. He brought me up also out of an horrible pit, out of the miry clay, and set my feet upon a rock, and established my goings"* (Ps. 40:1-2).

RIGHTEOUSNESS UNTO HOLINESS

The heading presents the same principle as *"iniquity unto iniquity,"* but in the very opposite direction.

First of all, Paul is telling the believer that since the power of the sin nature is broken, he no longer has to yield his physical members to unrighteousness. He can now yield them as slaves to righteousness unto holiness, that is, if the believer functions in God's way, which, as always, is the way of the Cross.

That's why Paul also said, *"Christ sent me not to baptize, but to preach the gospel: not with wisdom of words, lest the Cross of Christ should be made of none effect"* (I Cor. 1:17).

Paul was telling the Corinthians that they must not place anything over and above the Cross. In fact, he was telling the Corinthians, and all others, as well, and for all time, that the Cross of Christ is the gospel.

As iniquity unto iniquity dragged the person ever downward, despite all he could do otherwise, now the direction totally changes. Everything is ever upward. In other words, the righteousness goes into holiness—a holy life—and is a guarantee as the believer follows the divine nature, which is now within him and controlling him.

What we are now seeing, and what Paul is now explaining, is so beautiful as to defy description. It presents that which automatically comes with the born-again experience, providing the believer understands his proper place in Christ and what Christ did for him at the Cross. The whole wicked process of the fall is now reversed. This is God's way of salvation, of improving everything drastically, of giving life when there was nothing but death, and of giving blessing when there was nothing but sadness.

THE FALL

The tragedy about the fall is that the falling never reaches a stopping point. In other words, despite all the centuries of education, technological advancement, and higher learning, the fall continues even unto this hour, and will continue to continue. The actual truth is that man is experiencing the very opposite of the erroneous teaching of evolution. He is not gradually getting better, but he is getting worse—a direction that only God can reverse.

For example, the 20TH century has been the century of the greatest educational and technological advancements ever known to humanity, but at the same time, it has seen the greatest bloodletting of any century in history. In stark reality, the ever-deepening horror of the fall is made obvious to all who care to see. I state again that it is not possible for man to stop this downward slide within his own power or ability. That's the reason that man must be born again. Only God can stop this process, and only God can reverse the direction, and He does it exclusively through His Son, the Lord Jesus Christ. Any other hope is a fool's hope, and any other way is a fool's way.

FOR WHEN YOU WERE THE SERVANTS OF SIN

"For when you were the servants of sin, you were free from righteousness" (Rom. 6:20).

It should have been translated, even as we have stated, "For when you were the slaves of sin." There could be no state that is worse than the state of one who is a slave to sin. The pain and suffering that accompanies such bondage is actually beyond comprehension. There is no way that a person can break out of this trap (and a trap it is) by his own methodology or efforts. It simply cannot be done. Man has spent hundreds of billions of dollars trying to find a way out, but he is always unsuccessful.

Only God holds the solution!

Only God holds the way!

Thank God that untold millions have found that way down through the centuries, and it is still just as valid now as it was in centuries past. That way is the Cross of Christ.

Preachers who do not preach the Cross are preaching something, whatever it might be, that will set no captive free. With such a so-called gospel, no one will be released from satanic bondage, and no lives will be changed. It is the Cross alone that can effect the miracle of regeneration.

YOU WERE FREE FROM RIGHTEOUSNESS

Being a slave to sin precludes all righteousness. Of course, the type of righteousness of which Paul speaks is the righteousness of God.

Man has forever attempted to bring about his own righteousness. It is called self-righteousness. Let it be understood that any direction other than the Cross, no matter how religious it might be, will always and without fail conclude in self-righteousness. Sadly and regrettably, due to the fact that the modern church understands the Cross of Christ not at all as it regards sanctification, this particular church in this particular time frame is the most self-righteous that it has ever been, I think.

WHAT IS RIGHTEOUSNESS?

In the most simplistic terms, *righteousness* is simply that "which is right." However, it is God's definition of that which is right, and not that of man.

Man is forever attempting to bring about his own righteousness. It is called, as stated, self-righteousness. Man honors it, and so does most of the church, but not God. In fact, the great prophet Isaiah referred to such by saying, *"But we are all as an unclean thing, and all our righteousnesses are as filthy rags; and we all do fade as a leaf; and our iniquities, like the wind, have taken us away"* (Isa. 64:6).

Upon one's confession of faith in the Lord Jesus Christ, righteousness is freely and instantly imputed by God to the believing sinner. It comes only by faith and trust in Christ and what He has done for us at the Cross. It is given even to the worst of sinners, that is, if they properly believe Christ (Eph. 2:7-8).

However, if man attempts in any way to offer to God that which is of his own efforts, it will be rejected every time. Only the righteousness of God is acceptable.

FRUIT

"What fruit had you then in those things whereof you are now ashamed? for the end of those things is death" (Rom. 6:21).

The idea is that there is absolutely nothing of any value that can come out of the sinful experience. There is fruit all right, but it is evil fruit! Irrespective of the efforts, irrespective of the amount of money spent, and irrespective of education or anything else one might name, other than Christ, there is no proper fruit. That means zero!

To be ashamed is the right description. To be frank, the shame of such activity is always awful. Without God, it is a world of immorality, lying, cheating, stealing, war, hurt, pain, loneliness, sickness, suffering, and every imaginable evil thing. Any satisfaction that one gets in the world is fleeting and, consequently, soon gone. There is absolutely nothing that is positive or of any consequence in the world of sin, which is a world without Christ. It is only shame and disgrace.

FOR THE END OF THOSE THINGS IS DEATH

The heading proclaims again the ever deepening of the destructive power of iniquity unto iniquity. The end result is always death, that is, if one could speak of this horror of having an end, which one really cannot. The final result is the lake of fire, which will never end.

Death to one's marriage!

Death to one's business!

Death to one's physical body!
Death to friendships!
Death to security!
Death to life and living!

BUT NOW BEING MADE FREE FROM SIN

"But now being made free from sin, and become servants to God, you have your fruit unto holiness, and the end everlasting life" (Rom. 6:22).

We are made free from sin and free from the power of the sin nature because of what Jesus did at the Cross and our faith in Him and His finished work. That is the only way that we can have freedom from sin, meaning that sin no longer has dominion over us. It cannot be had any other way than through and by the Cross of Christ.

It doesn't require much on our part, only that our faith be exclusively in Christ and what He has done for us at the Cross. With that being done and maintained, the Holy Spirit will see to it that victory is ours. Otherwise, and no matter what the otherwise might be, bondage will most definitely be the end result.

Whatever we want to know about Christianity, whatever we want to know about the Bible, and whatever we want to know about the great doctrines of the Bible, all understanding, and I mean all, is found in the Cross of Christ. Once we understand that, once we abide by that, and once we put our faith exclusively in Christ and the Cross, and maintain it exclusively in

Christ and the Cross, everything will begin to fall into place. One will find that his understanding of the Word of God will greatly increase almost immediately once he begins to understand what I'm trying to teach you, and what the apostle Paul gave to us as it regards the Cross of Christ.

HOW?

As I write these words respecting the subject of the sin nature, I will at times look at material given by one of the greatest Greek scholars of the 20TH century. In his material, he told us what is to be done but not how it is done. The *how* is exclusively in the Cross. One might say that there are three things to this great fundamental of Christianity.

They are:

1. What Jesus did for us at the Cross.
2. Our faith in that finished work.
3. With that being done, the Holy Spirit will greatly and grandly help us, without which we simply cannot live this life.

Understanding this, the believer can be free now without having to go through a long regimen of religious works, which are of no value whatsoever. In other words, the terrible struggle that many believers are having with sin at this present time can be ended instantly, once and for all, exactly as Paul said: *"Now!"* Jesus meant what He said when He invited all to come to Him and rest (Mat. 11:28). He was speaking of rest from the struggle against sin.

AND BECOME SERVANTS TO GOD

The heading means "slaves to God, and not slaves to sin."

Allow me to say it again because Paul did: It is a privilege and a pleasure to be a slave of the Lord. Perhaps the word *slave* is an unfortunate metaphor for the simple reason that the term denotes a terrible state. However, where that is true with man, it is not true at all with God.

It is typified in the Old Testament by a slave who was given his freedom but loved his master so much, and felt that he was treated so grandly and so kindly, that he actually did not want his freedom. In all truth, he felt he had far more freedom serving his master than he would have had otherwise. He was granted protection and security, was given love, and was blessed constantly, so why would he want to leave that?

When he made this decision, *"He shall also bring him to the door, or unto the doorpost; and his master shall bore his ear through with an awl; and he shall serve him forever"* (Ex. 21:6; Deut. 15:17).

Spiritually speaking, I want both of my ears pierced with a spiritual awl for the simple reason that it is a privilege and an honor to serve and worship the Lord of glory—to be His servant, i.e., slave.

YOU HAVE YOUR FRUIT UNTO HOLINESS

Believers in every age have been called by God to be holy. There is no contradiction between the Old Testament and the

New Testament concept of holiness, but there is a change in emphasis of what holiness now involves.

The meaning of holiness is very near the meaning of sanctification, which simply means to be set apart from something to something. In this case, it is set apart from the world and all of its allurements exclusively to God.

The Greek word for holiness is *hagiasmos* and means "to purify, to consecrate, to sanctify."

Let us say it again: It means that we are to be set apart totally to God, that He guides our lives in every respect, and that we are swallowed up in His sweet will.

THE CROSS

Once again, if the believer places his or her faith exclusively in Christ and the Cross, and maintains it exclusively in Christ and the Cross, holiness will most definitely be the result. We must state again that it is impossible to understand the great doctrine of holiness unless we properly understand the Cross of Christ relative to our sanctification—how we live for God on a daily basis, and how we have victory over the world, the flesh, and the Devil. When one understands the Cross in this respect, and it's not difficult to understand at all, then one understands holiness.

At the moment that the believer places his or her faith exclusively in Christ and the Cross, and maintains it exclusively in Christ and the Cross, such a person is labeled as holy by God. In fact, there is nothing that one can do to make oneself holy except exercise faith in Christ and what He did for us at the Cross.

Religion has tried to perfect holiness by rules and regulations, by legalism, and by particular works, which God will never accept. Once again, it is faith alone, but we must understand that it has to be the correct object of faith, which is always the Cross.

Conversely, I don't care how much one studies holiness, sanctification, grace, the love of God, etc. Unless He understands the Cross of Christ relative to our everyday living for God, in other words, the part the Cross plays in all of this, he will never really understand the great rudiments of the faith, no matter how much he studies them. It's absolutely necessary for the believer to understand that everything we have is in Christ, with the giving of such made possible by the Cross. Once we understand that, and once we abide by that, everything else will begin to fall into place. In other words, by understanding and carrying out that, one will bring forth fruit unto holiness.

AND THE END EVERLASTING LIFE

Everlasting life or eternal life is the opposite of eternal death. Eternal life is eternal union with God by the cancellation of the eternal death penalty. Eternal life was brought about by the Cross and our faith in that finished work. Do you see now how that one begins to understand these great doctrines when one begins to understand the Cross of Christ relative not only to our salvation but, as well, to our sanctification?

Everlasting life is God's life infused in the believer. It is never our life if we are not dwelling in God. It is ours only when we get into Christ, and it is ours only as long as we abide in Him, which can only be done by the means of the Cross (I Jn. 2:24; 5:11-12). It is, therefore, something separate and apart from us, and it is imparted to us only when we are saved, and as long as we are saved. Christ is our life, and we have everlasting life as long as we have Him (Jn. 15:1-7; Col. 2:6-7; 3:4).

THE CONDITIONS

The conditions that Jesus lays down for entering into this life are faith in Him as the one mediator of the life, and the following of Him in a life of obedience, once again, all made possible by the Cross. The Lord alone knows the Father and can reveal Him to others (Mat. 11:27). Christ alone can give true rest and can teach men how to live and give them the power to live that which He teaches (Mat. 11:28). The sure way to this life is *"follow Me."* In other words, Jesus Christ is not only the bearer of everlasting life but, as well, its source.

Let us say it again: Union with Christ and all that He gives to us, all and without exception, is made possible by the Cross of Christ. While Jesus is the source, the Cross is the means by which everlasting life (in fact, all things) is given to us. It is the Cross that makes it all possible.

The believing sinner coming to Christ understands none of this at all, as should be obvious. He just simply believes Christ and he is saved; however, after one comes to the Lord, the Holy Spirit comes into such a heart and life and always, and without fail, will point us to the Cross of Christ, which makes everything possible.

THAT DONE BY CHRIST

Before the Cross, the Holy Spirit could not come into the hearts and lives of believers, no matter how dedicated they were, except only a few to help them carry out the task assigned them. When that was done, the Holy Spirit would leave. It was this way because the blood of bulls and goats could not take away sins. So, the sin debt remained and was taken away only by the Cross—what Jesus there did. What did He there do?

In the giving of Himself as a sacrifice (that's what it was), first of all and foremost, He atoned for all sin—past, present, and future—at least for all who will believe (Jn. 3:16; Col. 2:10-15; Gal. 6:14; I Cor. 2:2).

Second, Jesus satisfied the demands of the broken law. That demand was death, which means eternal separation from God and in the lake of fire forever and forever. However, upon simple faith in Christ and what He did for us at the Cross, the slate is wiped clean, so to speak, and we are immediately transferred from the position of lawbreaker to the position of law keeper. Once again, it's the Cross that is the means by which all of this is done. When we speak of the Cross, we aren't speaking of the wooden beam on which Jesus died, but rather what He there accomplished.

LIFE

The fullest and richest teachings regarding life are found in John's gospel. Actually, the greatest word of this gospel is *life*.

John says he wrote the gospel in order that *"you might have life"* (Jn. 20:31). In fact, most of the teachings of Jesus that are recorded circle around this great word *life*. This teaching is in no way distinctive and different from that of the other Gospels, but it is supplementary and completes the teaching of Jesus on the subject. The use of the word is not as varied, being concentrated on the one supreme subject.

John's gospel represents Jesus—the Logos—as the origin and means of all life to the world, which was made possible by the Cross. As the preincarnate Logos, He was and is the source of life, not only to mankind but, as well, to the universe (Jn. 1:4). Again we state that it was all made possible by the Cross.

As the incarnate Logos, He said His life had been derived originally from the Father (Jn. 5:26; 6:57; 10:18).

He then was and is the means of life to men (Jn. 3:15 16; 4:14; 5:21, 39-40).

This was the purpose for which He came into the world (Jn. 6:33-34, 51; 10:10), and even at the risk of being overly repetitive, it was all made possible by the Cross.

The nearest approach to the definition of eternal life is found in John 17:3, and is in a prayer of Jesus: *"And this is life eternal, that they might know You the only true God, and Jesus Christ, whom You have sent."*

THE WAGES OF SIN IS DEATH

"For the wages of sin is death; but the gift of God is eternal life through Jesus Christ our Lord" (Rom. 6:23).

The heading speaks of spiritual death, which is separation from God, and is the lot of those who follow this precarious path. On that broad way, there are no exceptions.

The word *wages* in the Greek is *opsoniom* and means "whatever is bought or purchased to be eaten with bread, such as fish, etc." It actually had reference to a Roman soldier and him being paid partially in money and partially in foodstuff. So, Paul is saying that sin does pay, but its wages is death. It is not a very pleasant prospect, to say the least!

It should be noticed that death is most always added to sin. As someone has well said, "All sin is a form of insanity in some way." That may sound drastic, but it happens to be true. Whatever direction it takes, sin always, and without exception, leads to death.

It can mean the death of a marriage, the death of one's ability, the death of well laid plans, and above all, spiritual death—this means separation from God forever and forever, which means eternal hell forever and forever.

BUT THE GIFT OF GOD IS ETERNAL LIFE THROUGH JESUS CHRIST OUR LORD

The heading says it all! It is the totality of things in this one verse.

However, the life that is eternal is found only through Jesus Christ our Lord, which is made possible by the Cross.

In all of this, Paul speaks of servants (or slaves) of iniquity, who lead a life of uncleanliness up beside the servants of righteousness, who lead a life of sanctification. As long, therefore, as a man is the servant of the one, he cannot obey the other. The one service is shameful and ends in death; the other is pure and ends in life and, in reality, has no end.

This life is consciously eternal, and this death is also consciously eternal, with the one being set over against the other. To be dead is horrible; to be consciously dead is more horrible— much more! To be conscious that one is dead eternally and to be eternally conscious of the fact is the most horrible thing that one could begin to imagine.

THE BELIEVER

While the sinner does earn his wages, which is death, the believer does not earn eternal life. It is a free gift, even as Paul says in verse 23. It is from God and is all made possible by the Cross. Perhaps we might better say that its channel is Christ and His atoning work.

God reckons the believer in Christ to have died with Him. The believer is to reckon this to be true. He is dead to the sin nature, to self, and to the world, and cannot, therefore, live in that to which He has died.

The believer is associated with Christ in His death, His burial, and His resurrection, and so is freed from the dominion of sin. He now becomes totally associated and totally linked, in fact, in Christ in His risen life and, consequently, becomes the bondslave of righteousness, and gladly so.

In the death and resurrection of Christ, we are liberated from the one master—sin—in order to be handed over to the other master—righteousness. It is in that risen life that the believer really knows Christ and experientially proves His power to sanctify Him wholly. Please allow me to say it one more time: It is all because of the Cross.

Oh let your soul now be filled with gladness
Your heart redeemed, rejoice indeed!

Oh may the thought banish all your sadness,
That in His blood you have been freed.

It is a good, every good transcending,
That Christ has died for you and me!

It is a gladness that has no ending
Therein God's wondrous love to see.

REFERENCES

CHAPTER 1

Wuest, Kenneth S. Wuest's Word Studies from the Greek New Testament: For the English Reader. Grand Rapids: Eerdmans, 1997.

Williams, George. The Complete Bible Commentary. Grand Rapids, MI, United States: Kregel Publications, U.S., 2008. Print. Pg. 858

Williams, George. The Complete Bible Commentary. Grand Rapids, MI, United States: Kregel Publications, U.S., 2008. Print. Pg. 856

The Pulpit Commentary: Romans. Ed. H. D. M. Spence-Jones. The Pulpit Commentary. London; New York: Funk & Wagnalls Company, 1909.

Williams, George. The Complete Bible Commentary. Grand Rapids, MI, United States: Kregel Publications, U.S., 2008. Print. Pg. 857

CHAPTER 2

Wuest, Kenneth S. *Wuest's Word Studies from the Greek New Testament: For the English Reader. Grand Rapids: Eerdmans, 1997.*

Williams, George. *The Complete Bible Commentary. Grand Rapids, MI, United States: Kregel Publications, U.S., 2008. Print. Pg. 857*

CHAPTER 3

The Pulpit Commentary: Romans. Ed. H. D. M. Spence-Jones. The Pulpit Commentary. London; New York: Funk & Wagnalls Company, 1909.

Wuest, Kenneth S. *Wuest's Word Studies from the Greek New Testament: For the English Reader. Grand Rapids: Eerdmans, 1997.*

CHAPTER 4

Williams, George. *The Complete Bible Commentary. Grand Rapids, MI, United States: Kregel Publications, U.S., 2008. Print. Pg. 858*

Wuest, Kenneth S. *Wuest's Word Studies from the Greek New Testament: For the English Reader. Grand Rapids: Eerdmans, 1997.*

CHAPTER 5

Strong, James. Enhanced Strong's Lexicon. Woodside Bible Fellowship, 1995.

Wuest, Kenneth S. Wuest's Word Studies from the Greek New Testament: For the English Reader. Grand Rapids: Eerdmans, 1997.

CHAPTER 6

Wuest, Kenneth S. Wuest's Word Studies from the Greek New Testament: For the English Reader. Grand Rapids: Eerdmans, 1997.

CHAPTER 8

Wuest, Kenneth S. Wuest's Word Studies from the Greek New Testament: For the English Reader. Grand Rapids: Eerdmans, 1997.

ABOUT EVANGELIST JIMMY SWAGGART

The Rev. Jimmy Swaggart is a Pentecostal evangelist whose anointed preaching and teaching has drawn multitudes to the Cross of Christ since 1955.

As an author, he has written more than 50 books, commentaries, study guides, and The Expositor's Study Bible, which has sold more than 3.2 million copies.

As an award-winning musician and singer, Brother Swaggart has recorded more than 50 gospel albums and sold nearly 17 million recordings worldwide.

For more than six decades, Brother Swaggart has channeled his preaching and music ministry through multiple media venues including print, radio, television and the Internet.

In 2010, Jimmy Swaggart Ministries launched its own cable channel, SonLife Broadcasting Network, which airs 24 hours a day to a potential viewing audience of more than 1 billion people around the globe.

Brother Swaggart also pastors Family Worship Center in Baton Rouge, Louisiana, the church home and headquarters of Jimmy Swaggart Ministries.

Jimmy Swaggart Ministries materials can be found at **www.jsm.org**.

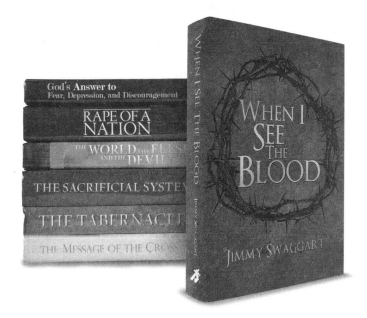